Practical Ballistics

Practical Ballistics

AN INTRODUCTORY GUIDE FOR RIFLE AND SHOTGUN SHOOTERS

LEWIS POTTER

THE CROWOOD PRESS

First published in 2014 by
The Crowood Press Ltd
Ramsbury, Marlborough
Wiltshire SN8 2HR

www.crowood.com

© Lewis Potter 2014

British Library Cataloguing-in-Publication Data
A catalogue record for this book is available from the British Library.

ISBN 978 1 84797 737 3

Disclaimer
The author and the publisher do not accept any responsibility in any manner whatsoever for any error or omission, or any loss, damage, injury, adverse outcome, or liability of any kind incurred as a result of the use of any of the information contained in this book, or reliance upon it. If in doubt about any aspect of ballistics readers are advised to seek professional advice.

All images are by the author except where otherwise stated.

Designed and typeset by Guy Croton Publishing Services, Tonbridge, Kent

Printed and bound in India by Replika Press Pvt Ltd

Contents

Acknowledgements

A book, especially with technical content, is rarely the work of one individual and most authors are only too glad of help, advice and assistance offered by others, from reviewing the manuscript to help with practical testing.

I therefore acknowledge the kind help and assistance from the staff of the Birmingham Proof House, the Greensleeves Shooting Club, Paul Edmunds, Paul Harding, Patrick and Paul Faulkner, Alan Cox, Geoff Paskin, Martin Taylor and my son, Dan Walker. Special thanks go to Chris Price, who, for the third time, volunteered to review a manuscript for me; also Derek Allsop and Dr Geoffrey Kolbe, who gave invaluable advice; I also appreciate the kind help given by Eley Hawk Ltd.

I am, as always, extremely grateful to my wife, Sue, who, for this fifth book of mine, has worked so hard converting my ever-increasingly scruffy handwriting into a legible typed manuscript.

I hope I have not failed to thank anyone, but if I have please accept my apologies as any such oversight will be down to my deficient memory, which I find does not improve with age.

Preface

The idea behind this book was to make the fairly complex world of ballistics easier to understand, and to relate in a practical manner to the kind of use the sportsman or target shooter has for their rifle and ammunition. It is nonetheless a subject that does require a degree of calculation, hence the fairly simple formulae included to enhance understanding of the principles involved.

If there is a single conclusion from these writings it is that there is no such thing as the perfect all-round cartridge, although some may come close for general target and live game use. However, when it comes to bullet design it is a very different matter, and we are drawn inevitably to accept that different designs can have widely different applications to perform at their best. So often it is a case of 'horses for courses'.

I have included reference to black powder firearms and the associated large calibre heavy bullets, as they have their uses even in a world dominated by high velocities and pointed bullets. The older technology tends to be a neglected subject, which I feel is a shame as it is all of interest and the basis of what was to come later.

In the same manner it was most useful, I believed, to include ballistic matters concerning the smooth-bored shotgun. All too often rifled and smooth-bored firearms are treated at different subjects, although a lot of shooters use both. I trust I have made the world of ballistics a little easier to understand and especially the practical application. That, however, is for you, the reader, to judge.

LASP 2013

Chapter 1
The Bullet and Cartridge

Pure ballistics tends to be thought of as a dry subject typified by complex formulae, the sort of specialization once described as knowing more and more about less and less. This is a little unkind perhaps, and some understanding of basic calculations is essential to have a reasonable comprehension of the subject, but what many shooters want to know is on a very practical level, such as 'if I alter A, how does it affect B?' – quite simply, what factors affect performance and accuracy. These can be many, apart from the obvious, such as rifling type and twist rate, bullet form and weight, right through the gamut of problems including head space, deformed cartridge cases and misshapen bullets.

Therefore this book is mainly about the practical aspects of ballistics: what affects performance and how to improve that, while hopefully avoiding some of the pitfalls. To get a better understanding of this it is first useful to know something of the development of the bullet and cartridge.

BASIC MUZZLE-LOADING FORMS

The bullet was at first a simple lead ball, its accuracy of manufacture limited by the precision or otherwise of the mould and the skill of the maker. Having examined old ball moulds one comes to the conclusion that it was, for many years, an imperfectly formed but nonetheless practical projectile, simply the best there was in the early days of firearms development. Just when the ball originated is difficult to establish, but it has probably been in use for around seven centuries as it is still used today.

In its early use in smooth-bore guns the ball would sit either directly against the propellant (black) powder, or between an over-powder wad or wadding with a further wad on top of the ball to prevent it rolling out of the barrel if the gun were held with the muzzle at a depressed angle. An alternative to this would have been to wrap the ball in a cloth patch to make it a snug fit in the bore, which, as we shall see in a later chapter, can have a remarkably detrimental effect on accuracy.

While originally the propellant gun powder (black powder) was held in bulk in a separate container typically made from wood or horn and later copper or brass, one quick loading development (a relative term) was individual powder charges in stoppered containers. This effectively was the start of the evolution of the cartridge, and was followed by the first almost self-contained cartridge with the ball at one end of a sealed paper tube and the powder behind it. The British used this system for the famous .75in-calibre flintlock musket affectionately known as Brown Bess.

The procedure was to bite or tear off paper from the cartridge and pour a small quantity of powder into the pan, close it, then pour the rest down the barrel followed by ramming home the ball in its paper tube that then acted as wadding. Reputedly some four shots a minute could be achieved with much practice where volume of fire, not accuracy, was the most desirable attribute.

The problem with a rifled muzzle-loading firearm is that ideally the ball needs to be sized to fully engage the rifling at the breech end of the barrel. This means hard work loading, including the use of a mallet on the ramrod or a short starter rod to get the ball to engage the rifling at the muzzle. Then there are other complications, such as most muzzle-loading barrels would have been finished prior to the addition

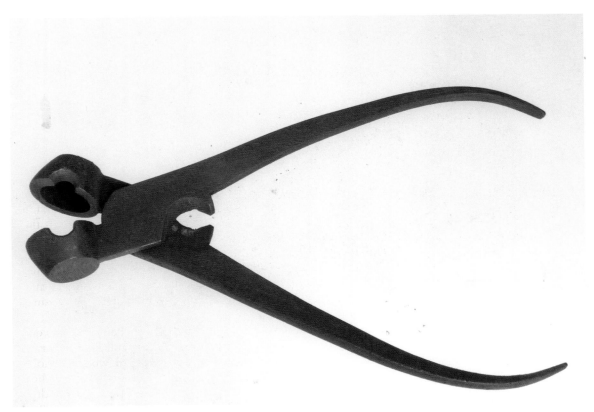

Scissor ball mould. The cutter for removing the casting sprue that gives this type of mould its name is just at the rear of the pivot pin.

of the rifling by a process known as spill boring. Spill boring produces a tapered bore, the amount dependent upon the number of passes of the tool, how much material is removed, and the length of the barrel, but this taper can vary from a few tenths of thousandths of an inch to two to three thousandths.

It was believed, and appears to be the case with low velocity arms, that the slightly tapered or choked bore was beneficial to accuracy, the only complication here being that the breech end is, of course, then going to be larger than at the muzzle. This means the ball will not be such a precise fit, even if engaged nicely in the rifling at the muzzle, and the force required to start the ball can make it out of round and therefore ballistically inefficient.

Speed of loading and reloading, especially for military purposes, is always an issue, and one crude method occasionally resorted to was to use a calibre-sized ball ('calibre' being the bore size prior to the addition of the rifling) that would slide down the barrel without engaging the rifling. Once seated against the powder, a hard blow or two with a steel ramrod would partially expand the ball sideways into the rifling. This had the twin disadvantages of compressing the gun powder into a virtually solid mass, which is not an aid to good, consistent ignition, and once again producing a deformed ball that will not fly as true as a spherical one.

The answer, as so often is the case, was stunningly simple – the patched ball. This works well in a rifled firearm with the slightly undersized ball, the lubricated patch gripping the rifling while protecting the ball. On firing, the patch falls away as it leaves the muzzle while the unmarked ball spins its way to the target. With a comparatively light ball, as compared to a conical bullet, the rifling twist can be fairly slow,

For years powder was carried in a separate container. This is a fairly late Hawkesley-made leather-over-copper powder flask, the adjustable nozzle graduated in grains for rifle use.

which is another aid to loading as it causes less resistance than a faster rate of twist. In many ways, crude as this technology may seem when viewed from the perspective of the twenty-first century, it was the origin of the jacketed bullet.

One of the advantages of rifling is its ability to handle conical-nosed bullets with a long cylindrical body and therefore of greater weight than a ball of the same calibre. This has many advantages, including a more ballistically efficient shape, greater muzzle energy, more retained energy at longer ranges, and better terminal performance with its superior sectional density (ratio of diameter to length). The problems of loading involving the rifled muzzle loader are much the same as when using a ball, but somewhat more exaggerated.

For the target shooter, where time was of far less consequence, one answer was the paper patched bullet. This was achieved by attaching to the muzzle while loading, a smooth-bore 'false muzzle' cut to accommodate strips of overlapping paper; the bullet was placed over the paper, and was then pushed or rammed into the bore. Like this the paper forms a jacket around the bullet, and in the same way as the patched ball, grips the rifling, then falls away, rather like a sabot, when the bullet leaves the muzzle.

The disadvantage with this system was the time needed for careful loading, and on a windy day it must have been quite challenging keeping all those strips of paper in place before entering the bullet into the false muzzle. As was so often the case for centuries, the prime mover in firearms development is advancement in efficiency in weapons of war, meaning firepower, so something less fussy was required.

Ball and lubricated patch, the first step towards the jacketed bullet.

THE MECHANICALLY FITTED BULLET

There are two well known candidates in this category: Colonel John Jacob's winged bullet (not the first of its type, but the final and most successful development), and Sir Joseph Whitworth's hexagonal bullet. The former has projecting lugs that engage the rifling so the body of the bullet can be calibre size, which again is a great aid to loading. Once again, however, from our perspective it may seem odd that someone should design a bullet with effectively short, stubby paddles sticking out on either side, inevitably creating turbulence as the bullet spins through the air.

To a certain extent it was a case of 'needs must', where a degree of accuracy was offset against efficiency of loading. Also, at subsonic velocities and with comparatively slow rates of rifling twist, slight imperfections in bullet design or construction tend to have a lesser effect than with bullets driven at supersonic speeds. Thus Jacob's bullet seems to have found its niche in larger calibre rifles such as those used for dangerous game usually shot at short range.

Whitworth's hexagonal bullet looks like a blunt-nosed, slightly twisted piece of hexagon bar which is formed to mate with the hexagonal rifling. An idea also applicable to artillery shells, in small arms it became a favourite once again of the long-range target shooters. Such was the fame of the Whitworth rifle that the Birmingham firm of Parker-Hale reintroduced it as one of their range of modern muzzle-loading rifles. However, while their Enfield rifles were manufactured to the original gauges, the

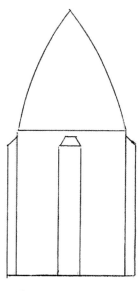

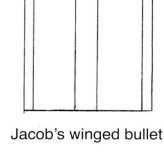

Jacob's winged bullet

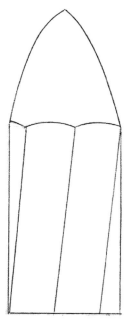

Whitworth's hexagonal bullet

Mechanically fitted bullets. Jacob's winged bullet was originally designed with four lugs, later two, that engaged into deep-cut rifling. Whitworth's hexagonal bullet fitted rifling of the same form.

Whitworth '.451 Volunteer' was not quite the same as an original, even if a worthy effort.

The Minié Bullet

The great breakthrough which gave speed of loading and acceptable accuracy was the invention of what is popularly known as the minié bullet, another of those ideas of brilliant simplicity that crop up from time to time. The principle of a comparatively loose-fitting bullet that would expand to grip the rifling as a result of the pressure applied by the burning propellant was first experimented with as early as 1823, and over the next thirty years or so there were several variations in design culminating in a simple hollow base design that was actually an improvement on the minié of 1849.

The great advantage of this type of bullet in a muzzle loader is that it can be loaded as quickly as a smooth-bore musket but has the accuracy inherent in a rifled firearm. Almost at a stroke the smooth-bore musket became obsolete, and the next need was for a practical breech-loading system.

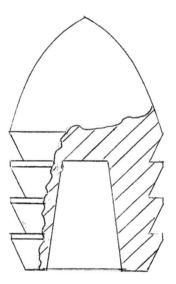

The minié bullet and its variants revolutionized loading a rifle. The bullet has a large hollow base which at different times was fitted with an iron cup or wooden plug to aid expansion into the rifling.

LOADING AT THE BREECH

There were two significant steps forward concerning rifle accuracy and a greater appreciation of ballistics. The first was loading at the breech, and the second was replacing the black powder with smokeless propellant, which produced considerably less fouling of the bore. Even though by the late nineteenth century black powder was the very best of its type, and is hardly matched even today, the deposits after firing have an adverse effect on accuracy and

loading. While as a general rule this also varies with the quality of the powder, on a hot day, or when the barrel heats up with use, the burnt residue becomes crusty and hard, though less so on a cool, damp day. Nevertheless in all situations it means loading becomes progressively harder, especially with a muzzle loader, and it even affects breech loaders when it builds up in the lead into the rifling.

I once found problems when using a black powder breech loader in competition in a rapid fire stage with powder that was not of the best

A variety of bullet designs. From left: ball; cast lead with gas check; full metal jacket (FMJ) cutaway to show the turn-over at the base; cutaway target hollow point – the jacket covering the base.

quality. After a few shots the occasional 'flyer' was recorded on the target, well outside the rest of the group. After twelve shots one of these flyers became so unstable in flight it emitted that distinctive buzzing sound as it tumbled down range. It seemed in this instance that the powder fouling had become sufficiently hard to tear the paper patching so badly that the bullet left the muzzle with insufficient spin to stabilize it. This seemed to be borne out by shooting the gun later and cleaning between shots, when good accuracy was restored.

Part of the problem could also be attributed to lack of bullet lubricant, because cast bullets with large lubrication grooves, rather than the grease wad (what the Americans call a grease 'cookie') behind a paper-patched bullet, performed much better with this particular black powder. Still, it was an interesting lesson in how other matters can affect quite basic ballistics, even with good bullets and excellent rifling. For centuries, though, black powder as a propellant held back the development of smaller bore rifles

and the kind of higher muzzle velocities that could, finally, be obtained with smokeless powders.

With smokeless powder and jacketed bullets the world of shooting changed once again. Where previously .450in had been a medium calibre and .360in regarded as small, sizes around .30in calibre became the norm. Almost overnight velocities were up by around 50 per cent over the very best performing black powder loads, and nearly double many of the older loadings.

Loading at the breech also contributed greatly towards accuracy and more consistent ballistics. Although there had been experiments with breech loaders as early as the sixteenth century, it was never a truly practical proposition until the advent of the metallic cartridge. The capping breechloader led the way with its paper cartridge loaded at the breech, although it was still ignited by a percussion cap on a nipple mounted on the breech block. An early metallic cartridge rifle like the 1874 Sharps was a simple

The gyrojet: was this to be the future, essentially a rocket-propelled bullet? It was an interesting concept that did not catch on. It is shown here with a .303 British full metal jacket military bullet for size comparison.

redevelopment of the earlier capping breech loader, and, of course, was still fuelled by black powder.

However, put smokeless powder and the metallic cartridge together, and many things are possible, such as carefully designed jacketed bullets; and because there is such a lack of powder fouling, each shot is virtually consistently the same as the preceding, except sometimes when firing from a cold, clean barrel, or when it is overheated.

Higher velocities meant the adoption of jacketed bullets, at first called copper patched, following on from paper patched. The need, of course, for jacketing was that without it even hard lead alloy bullets used at higher velocities would strip the rifling, depositing lead in the bore and having no spin

to impart stability. What might be described as a 'mini-jacket' is the gas check which fits over the base of a lead bullet to protect it from the hot, high pressure gases, especially those generated when using smokeless powders. Using a jacket means that the bullet is less prone to damage during handling; it also means that bullets with very precise manufacturing tolerances and a fine streamlined shape can perform better, especially at the longer ranges. The metallic cartridge as we know it had arrived.

That is not quite the end of the story, as inventors push ideas even further, such as caseless rounds, or that slightly crazy idea, the gyrojet, a sort of mini-rocket self-propelled bullet – perhaps rather a triumph of ingenuity over practicality.

THE METALLIC CARTRIDGE

For almost all of us, the metallic cartridge is the ultimate development of the cartridge in all its various modern and some not so modern forms. The basic types likely to be encountered are the recessed rim (more commonly called 'rimless'); the rebated rim, where the recessed rim is smaller than the main diameter of the body of the case; the belted, which is effectively a forward-located rim on a recessed rim case, which also provides useful reinforcing; and that oldie, the rimmed case. Although of all of these the rimmed case has been around the longest, it is by no means technically inferior when used for specialist applications such as break-open or falling block rifles. It is not well suited to magazine rifles, which are much in the majority –

hence the great popularity of the recessed rim cartridge.

With these cartridge cases two types of primer are in use, the most common and useful being the Boxer primer named after Colonel Edward Mounier Boxer, a British officer; this is a self-contained design sitting in the primer pocket. The American Hiram Berdan's system consists of a hollow cup with the anvil formed in the base of the primer pocket, and two flash holes either side. The Berdan is little used except mainly for military applications, and is of so little use to the keen hand loader that it can be discounted for practical purposes – although forty years ago we sometimes had to use it due to a lack of the older types of cartridge case.

In recent years the supply of cases for obsolete cartridges has improved enormously thanks to

The three common rim types: from left: rimless (recessed rim), rimmed and belted.

Contrefire cartridge case.

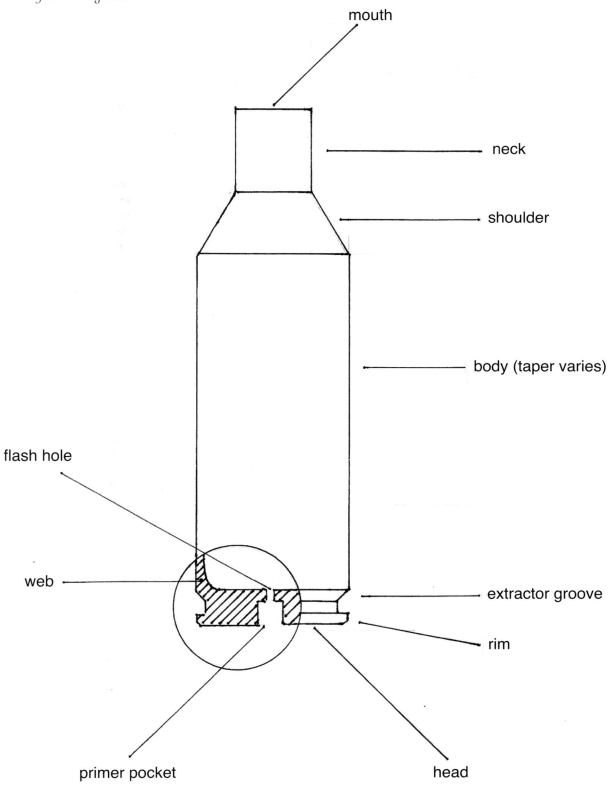

mouth

neck

shoulder

body (taper varies)

flash hole

web

extractor groove

rim

primer pocket

head

specialist makers, all of these modern supplies being Boxer primed regardless of how the originals were produced. Even the rimfire has had something of a revival. The .22 Winchester WMR, commonly referred to as the .22 magnum, was introduced in 1959, with the recent development of the rimfire cartridges being the .17 HMR.

TERMINOLOGY

To understand the basic principles concerning firearms and ballistics it is very useful, even essential, to have an appreciation of the correct terminology. The language relating to firearms is sometimes a little archaic. It has slowly evolved over the years very much at its own pace, and sometimes almost independent to mainstream English. One typical example is the British gunmaker or gunsmith referring to a turnscrew — what most people in the English-speaking world would describe as a screwdriver. The word 'turnscrew' was common in Victorian times, and while everyone else adopted the later description, the gun trade doggedly stuck with what they were familiar with, about a century out of step with the modern world but nonetheless demonstrating a charmingly old-fashioned way of dealing with progress.

Such old language is more common in the shotgun world, but even relating to the rifled firearm there can be confusion as to the correct descriptions and terminology. Partly to blame are internet chat sites and forums where it seems that participants, when they do not fully understand the subject, tend to adopt words that sound about right, or simply make things up. This is flashed around the world in seconds, and it is quite possible for information that might be untrue to be given credibility simply because it appears on the internet, which in itself is a wonderful tool when used correctly.

Therefore, for the purposes of this book, 'cartridge' is used as a generic term for both the metallic rifle cartridge and the paper- or plastic-cased shotgun cartridge. 'Bullet' is used for any elongated projectile, 'ball' is reserved for spherical bullets simply to distinguish between the two, while 'shot' describes multiple small pellets or balls as used in a shotgun.

Calibre and Gauge

To be strictly correct, 'calibre' is the bore of a rifle prior to the addition of rifling, with the exception of 'gauge' rifles, which are based on the old shotgun system of measurement. The use of the word 'calibre' has been extended in common usage over the years to describe not just the calibre, but also the cartridge a rifle is chambered for, and this has gone on to cause confusion so perhaps requires a bit more explanation. An example of this would be 'rifle calibre .270 Winchester'; however, to use it the other way around, as in '.270 Winchester calibre rifle', the use of calibre is then redundant, little more, in fact, than an affectation, as '.270 Winchester rifle' gives you all the information necessary.

Where it really starts to go wrong is when 'calibre' is used as a direct substitute for 'cartridges'. It is not unusual to come across a description like, say, the 30-06 Springfield cartridge described as 'a good old calibre dating from 1906'. It is, of course, a fine old cartridge, and the use of 'calibre' in this instance is quite wrong. There are plenty of others in .30 calibre, some predating it, some of later development, some not so good.

Those big old rifles, both muzzle and breech loaders, that may be referred to as 'gauge rifles' are based on the old spherical ball system of measurement common to shotguns and, at one time, cannons. With small arms the size referred to the number of spherical lead balls of bore diameter that go to make up one pound in weight. So it is easy to see that a spherical ball that is $\frac{1}{16}$lb means '16 gauge'. A large shotgun or rifle that accepts a lead ball weighing $\frac{1}{4}$lb, or four to the pound, is gauged at 4. Whether to use gauge or bore is another matter. The older system, which the Americans still tend to use, is gauge, while bore is most common in the UK — yet a gunsmith will still refer to 'gauging the bore'.

To use 'calibre' in this instance is not logical as it denotes a direct measurement, while what we actually have is a comparative measurement relating size to weight. Even that great showman of the British gun trade, W. W. Greener, was inclined to use terms such as 'calibre 12 bore', but in this instance I believe he was not actually at his technical best. One exception, of course, is the .410, which refers to a direct measurement or calibre.

For the sake of clarity I have used 'bore' to denote the size of gauge rifles and shotguns because, while the latter is probably the more technically proper, 'bore' is an acceptable substitute and is well established in the UK. 'Calibre' I have continued to use as meaning a bore measurement, rather than describing the cartridge for which a rifle is chambered.

Lead, Throat or Leed

The lead of the rifling is the tapered section in front of the chambered bullet that literally leads it into the full depth of rifling. There has, in the past, been some debate as to whether it should be spelt 'leed', which has tended to be the case with shotguns – and when a sentence or paragraph also includes lead, meaning the dense, soft metal that is the basis of most bullets, the usefulness of an alternative spelling becomes fairly obvious. However, 'lead', regardless of the possibility of confusion, of which there are plenty of examples in the English language, appears to be the established and recognized spelling when referring to this part of a rifle barrel.

So, is the lead the same as the throat? Some authorities would say yes: after all, when we wish to alter the lead we use a throating reamer; but it is another possible area of mild confusion if the two terms are used interchangeably. For the purposes of this book I have stayed with 'lead' as meaning the whole tapered section, and 'throat' just being the start of the rifling where erosion – or throat erosion – first becomes really visible.

Backstop / Backdrop

Reference will occasionally appear in the text to 'backstop', meaning a natural or artificial barrier used to arrest the bullet's flight within a certain distance, and referred to on a rifle range as a 'butt stop'. It is to be noted that 'backdrop' is being used increasingly on the internet and sporting press: however, the origin of 'backdrop' is the curtain at the rear of a theatre stage which would often carry a scenic picture. It may

also be correctly used to describe the actual scenery behind something that is the focal point of a picture, as in 'he was pictured with the Malvern Hills as a backdrop'. It is not what a backstop is to a rifle bullet, and I have included this explanation to avoid confusion, as the two terms are actually not interchangeable.

Rifle Action

Another area of slight confusion, before we get down to the real detail, relates to parts of a rifle. The word 'action', often used as a suffix as in 'bolt action' (but sometimes used on its own) is really meant to describe the complete working assembly of parts – bolt, receiver, firing pin, springs, cocking piece – and how it functions. One sometimes hears the receiver being described as the action, but it can be seen from the foregoing that this is not actually correct: it is only one part, although a major pressure-containing part, along with the bolt and barrel.

Things become slightly more confusing with the traditional hinged break-open rifles, whether double or single barrelled, where the large part that the barrels lock on to is the 'body' or 'action body'. In British gunmaking terms this description would also be applied to a falling block rifle, the main parts, therefore, being the body and breech block. As these terms have become fairly standardized I have used 'receiver' to describe the main component of a bolt action, but 'body' where it is both correct and appropriate to apply it to other, older types of rifle and shotguns.

The Riflescope

One cannot deal with rifle-related matters without mention at some time of sights, and the common arrangement on many rifles is the riflescope. This is really a specialist telescope, and many of the old hands who remember them starting to come into more common usage in the 1950s still refer to them as telescope sights. The description often applied now is 'telescopic' sights, and while a draw telescope such as favoured by a stalker on the hill is truly telescopic, there is some doubt in my mind whether it really is the appropriate word for the sight on a rifle. My preference is riflescope, a word possibly of American origin, but whichever way you look at it, a contraction of rifle-telescope, which I feel covers things quite neatly.

DETAILS OF BULLET DESIGN

Bullet design affects performance and is therefore an elementary part of ballistics. For anyone approaching this subject for the first time it must seem incredibly confusing. Basic types include spire point, round nosed, flat nosed – sometimes called flat point even though it is a contradiction in terms – hollow point, full metal jacket – at one time called full patch bullets – boat-tail, semi-jacketed and cast (lead). Subtle detail design features can make some of these appear quite different to each other by exposing more or less lead at the point, adding a ballistic tip, anti-friction coating or cannelure, or being produced from solid copper.

All bullets, though, will have some of the following in common. Take, for instance, the standard military .303 British full metal jacket bullet as a typical example that displays all the basic features. Starting at the 'pointy end', a non-technical but easily understood description, we have the meplat, ogive, cannelure; then there is some slight confusion, as the main part is described variously as the body, bearing surface or sometimes bourrelet; then, approaching the base, we have the heel. Since most of these words appear to have their origins in old French architectural terms, I think 'bourrelet', for the main body of the bullet, has some historical claim, but it is also sometimes used to describe the major diameter at (or behind) the ogive, not including any driving bands. So for our purposes, 'bearing surface' is probably the most widely recognized term and the most useful.

Note that driving bands are a feature of some cast lead bullets in the form of a raised section incorporating grease grooves to hold lubricant. In this sort of design the bourrelet is calibre size, with only the driving bands engaging the rifling. Driving bands may also be found on solid bronze or copper bullets designed, in this instance, to reduce the area of bearing surface in contact with the barrel in an effort to keep friction and pressures within manageable limits.

Even cast bullets vary, the most obvious differences being between those with visible lubrication grooves and paper patched. They can also be found coated with a lubricant and without the deep grooves, hollow based – rather like a minié – or bore riding, a type with a long nose of calibre diameter, the rear part of the bullet with lubrication grooves being the only part that engages the rifling.

To the untutored eye the most visible differences in bullet design occur with the ogive. Ogive means 'pointed arch', and if you look at a church window or something similar one can see the similarity. With a bullet the radius of the ogive is normally expressed in calibres, so for example our .303 bullet shown has an ogive that is seven calibres' radius; the more pointed it is, the larger the radius and therefore multiples of the calibre. Extending back from this to the minimum, which is half the radius, the ogive then is not a pointed arch but becomes a plain arch – what we recognize as a round-nosed bullet.

It does not end there, as we have two radius forms of ogive: the tangent ogive, which is the most common, and the secant ogive, which is used on some spire point bullets. In simple terms, the tangent ogive is a radius formed from a multiple of the calibre taken from a line at right angles to a point where the ogive joins the bearing surface. The secant ogive is twice the tangent radius.

Then we have to add in some of the VLD (very low drag) bullets to help complete the picture. Here we encounter bullets where the head of the bullet is very long and can appear to be a straight taper, rather as you produce when sharpening a pencil with the traditional school sharpener. In actual fact it is usually of ogival form, but sometimes in excess of 15-calibre radius, which visually gives little impression of a curved form.

Head and Noses

The front part of the bullet, whatever its actual shape, back to the point where it joins the bearing surface, is generally described either as the

OPPOSITE: *Details of bullet design.*

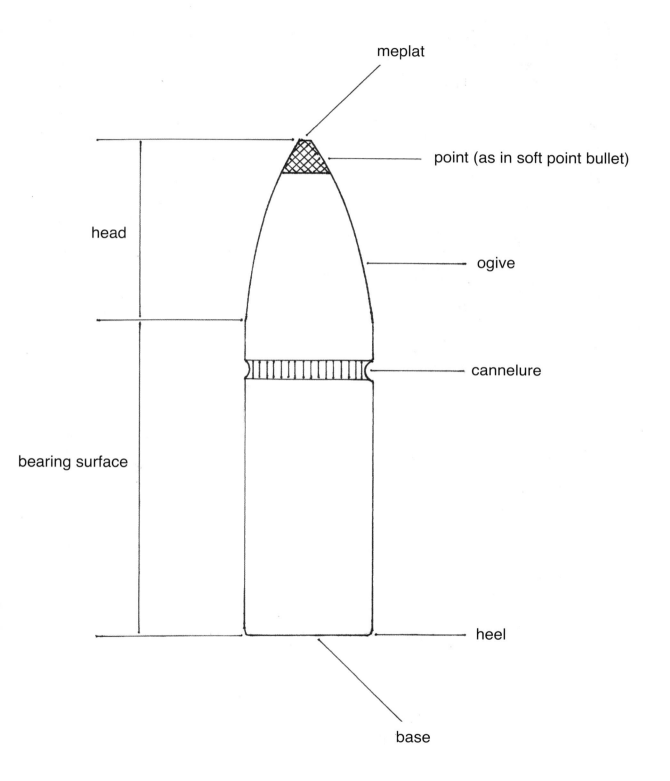

meplat

point (as in soft point bullet)

head

ogive

cannelure

bearing surface

heel

base

bullet shown with tangent ogive of 2.5 calibres radius

There are many examples of the ogival form; here is one from nature, the jawbone of a bowhead whale set up as a decorative arch in a park.

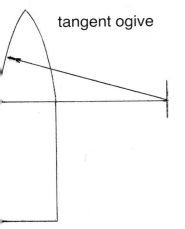

tangent ogive

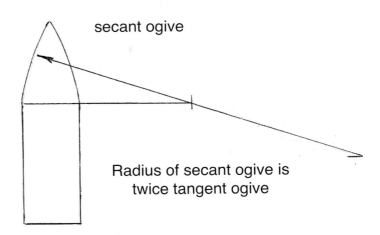

secant ogive

Radius of secant ogive is
twice tangent ogive

The difference between the tangent and secant ogives.

'nose' or the 'head' of the bullet. Some manufacturers appear to use 'nose' when all that is meant is the exposed lead of a 'soft-nosed' bullet, while others use it to mean the complete head. I favour the former, where 'nose' is the area around and just behind the tip or meplat, and 'head' is the whole shape back to the bearing surface.

This is not the same as 'bullet head', or even just 'head', when what is meant is 'bullet'. While these sorts of descriptive term do sometimes appear in the sporting press and in advertisements (where metallic cartridges may be listed as 'bullets' and the range of cartridges as 'calibres'), they are slang terms that have no legitimacy.

Bullets are designed for specific purposes, and what the woodland stalker finds useful at those short ranges for a clean kill is not the same as what the 1,000yd target shooter needs for the best performance. In fact it is easy for the short range, live game shooter to become obsessed with accuracy when realistically a bullet that gives very good terminal performance and acceptable, consistent accuracy is often what is actually required. Nor do we always need to become too concerned about ballistic coefficient for short range use. Many big bullets intended for dangerous game have, compared to the best target bullets, appalling drag through the air because of their blunt shape, but at distances often measured in tens of yards it does not matter: what would matter is stopping the buffalo that is perhaps intent on your demise.

What I am saying here is that theory is fine, but the answer may depend upon which direction you approach the problem. The oft-quoted expression that the only interesting rifle is an accurate rifle is certainly a most desirable goal, but in practice accuracy may turn out to be a relative term, and what holds true for a .22 centre-fire is not necessarily the same for a .600 Nitro Express: something about horses for courses comes to mind.

So, let us now look at the ballistics that affect performance and accuracy.
* For further information on nomenclature please refer to full details in the glossary at the end of this book.

A wide variety of bullets. From left: soft nose with heavy jacket, cannelure and small amount of lead exposed for expansion and good penetration; hollow point, boat-tail target bullet; bullet with polymer tip; solid bronze big game bullet intended for very deep penetration; .50 calibre very low drag (VLD) bullet; cast bore-riding bullet; paper-patched bullet and military full metal jacket (FMJ).

Chapter 2
Internal Ballistics and Associated Matters

Internal ballistics are those matters that affect performance while the bullet is still in the barrel, and this is not separate to external ballistics but is part of the whole matter of ballistic performance. In fact, internal ballistics are the foundation for everything that follows, especially that matter of greatest concern to most rifle enthusiasts, consistent accuracy. A variety of things comes into play that all have an influence on what happens from the moment the firing pin hits the primer, and there are also other contributory factors such as rifle construction and, as part of that, lock time. The former is mainly a matter outside the scope of this book, but that of lock time is worth some consideration.

LOCK TIME

Lock time is simply the small delay between squeezing the trigger and the sear releasing the firing pin to the time taken for it to strike the primer. Therefore it follows that the longer this delay, the more chance there is of the user introducing an error in aiming. Although this is a shooter-related matter, the end result on the target might suggest a ballistic fault, and eliminating human error when testing rifles and cartridges is often the biggest challenge to obtaining accurate results.

With most modern bolt actions lock time is commendably short as compared to the older generation of rifles such as the Mauser M98 – although even modern rifles such as the Ruger No. 1 falling block, with a comparatively heavy hammer travelling through an arc, have a long lock time. At the same time it has to be said that, for the really practised and accomplished shot who is familiar with the rifle, errors due to differences in lock time are, perhaps, more theo-

retical than likely to have great detrimental effect. Anyway, lock time can usually be improved – in other words, reduced – by using lighter components, 'faster' springs, or by reducing the length of travel. However, these sorts of modification can only be taken so far before unreliable strikes cause misfires.

For the enthusiast who wants to look into this further there is a simple formula applicable to the bolt-action rifle to calculate lock time:

$$t = \sqrt{\frac{2ms}{f}}$$

Where t = time the firing pin takes to fall
s = length of firing pin travel
m = mass of firing pin + ½ the mass of spring
f = spring performance weight

Practical tests have shown the following:

When considering the total delay between the firer wishing to fire the shot and the projectile exiting the barrel, the total time = $t1 + t2 + t3 + t4 + t5$.

$t1$ = delay caused by the firer, and dependent on the firer and his experience; it is usually taken as being between 40 and 60 milliseconds (ms).
$t2$ = trigger mechanism delay*.
$t3$ = firing mechanism delay*.
$t4$ = propellant ignition time; this is usually taken to be between 1 and 3ms.
$t5$ = projectile time in the barrel; this is calculated from the average velocity whilst the projectile is in the barrel, not the muzzle velocity. A good approximation is to use half the muzzle velocity.
* Note: There is considerable difference between figures for modern sporting or target rifles, military-based actions (e.g. Lee Enfield,

Mauser M98), and vintage designs such as those with large side hammers.

Firearms designers concentrate on reducing t2 and t3 because these are the only ones they have control over and are a significant part of the total.

IGNITION AND BARREL TIME

Consider that there are two basics to contend with: ignition time and barrel time. Ignition time is the interval between the firing pin striking the primer and the bullet starting to move forwards. For most practical purposes with small arms cartridges it is an insignificant amount of time, but with some of the really big punt gun (shotgun) cartridges it may be an advantage to initiate ignition at the front of the powder charge to get better and more uniform powder burn with the type of coarse-grained black powder often used.

With regard to barrel time, when firing a bullet it does not just have to engage and pass through the rifling, but must accelerate from nought to its muzzle velocity in a fraction of a second. If we look at a 30 calibre barrel as an example, this has a true calibre size of 0.300in and rifling cut 0.004in deep, so the maximum diameter to the bottom of the rifling grooves is 0.308in. The bullet that fits will be 0.308in diameter, but may be up to 0.001in smaller, depending upon the manufacture. Either way, it is a good interference fit in the rifling, as anyone who has had to remove a bullet stuck part-way up a barrel can confirm.

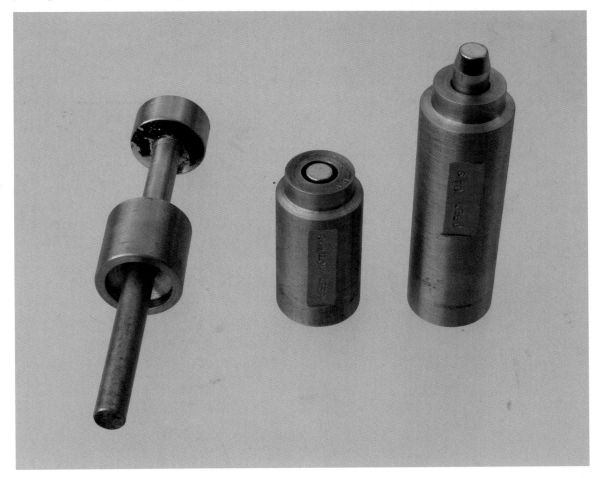

Jigs for testing rifling engraving pressure. From left: guide and push rod; centre jig with long shallow lead (note position of the bullet); jig with standard lead.

A jig in the hydraulic press.

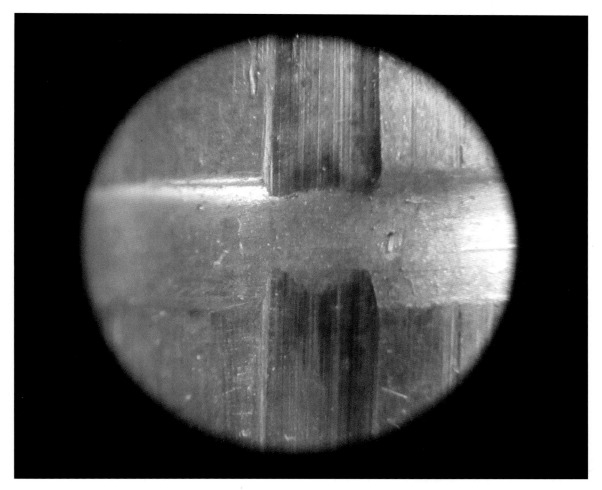

Close-up of the rifling mark on a bullet (× 24).With the naked eye rifling marks on a bullet appear smooth and shiny. This close-up shows how the jacket has been reformed across the cannelure, the rifling leaving small score marks.

If the velocity with which the bullet escapes from the muzzle of a 24in (60cm) barrel is 2,800ft (853m)/sec, then from rest this has been achieved in just under one thousandth of a second. Muzzle-velocity figures in the region of 3,500ft (1,067m)/sec will drop barrel time to around 0.0006sec, while those long-barrelled, big black-powder rifles with bullets pushed out at comparatively modest subsonic velocities, will have a typical barrel time in the region of 0.002sec – still much faster than the human senses can comprehend.

This helps to explain why, for medium to high velocities, pressures in the region of 15 tons/square inch are necessary – and it is always worth remembering that this is all happening just in front of your face and between your hands, and when things go wrong they can go badly wrong in almost an instant of time.

Experiment

The following experiment was to indicate the force required to push a .30 calibre bullet into the rifling (rifling engraving pressure).

Equipment

A length of rifle barrel with lead cut, guide for the push rod, push rod, hydraulic pump with gauge, and a press jig.

Results

The average maximum reading on the gauge when the bullet starts to engage the rifling 435 pounds per square inch (psi).

The actual ram pressure based on the area of ram × indicated pressure 435psi × 0.687sq in = 298.7psi.

What now has to be accounted for is the ram pressure being transmitted to the base of a .30 calibre bullet with a surface area of only 0.0745sq in. This is like the stiletto heel effect, where even the weight of a dainty woman seems magnified on the small area of the shoe heel. Imagine, as an easy example, an inverted cone with 4lb (1.8kg) bearing on a top surface area of 4sq in (26sq cm), giving a distributed load of 1lb (300g) per square inch (6.5sq cm). If the bottom of the cone is only 1sq in (6.5sq cm), the load there is equivalent to 4 tons per square inch.

So, with our bullet the load is $\frac{\text{actual ram pressure}}{\text{bullet base surface area}}$

$= \text{pressure per square inch}$

$\frac{298.7}{0.0745} = 4009.4\text{psi}$

Or, for convenience, $\frac{\text{pounds per square inch}}{2240}$

$= \text{tons per square inch}$

$\frac{4009.4}{2240} = 1.789 \text{ tons per square inch (tsi)}$

This figure can only be a guide, as pushing it comparatively slowly under constant pressure is not quite the same as accelerating it into the bore at greatly increasing pressures. Also jacket material and bullet construction do have an effect (a thin copper jacket can, for example, be quite 'slippery'). However, it does give a good indication of the sort of pressure involved just to push the bullet to form it into the rifling, let alone accelerate it up the barrel to reach muzzle velocities often exceeding 2,800ft/sec (853m/sec).

This rifling engraving pressure is extremely important in determining the peak chamber pressure during the internal ballistic cycle, and is significantly affected by the lead angle. The steeper the lead angle, the greater the peak pressure, and it is worth remembering that the angle tends to decrease as the barrel wears.

What we cannot duplicate with an experiment like this is the tendency for a bullet to 'bump up' or expand radially due to the pressure at the base, nor can we include that feature described as 'bul-

let skid'. The fact that the bullet is trying to accelerate forwards in a straight line (without rotating) as it engages the rifling means it does not immediately locate cleanly into the rifling but is moving forwards at the same time as the front of the bearing surface is engaging the rifling.

This is visible as slightly distorted rifling grooves engraved in the bullet at the leading edge of the bearing surface, as compared to those nearer the base. It is more noticeable with revolvers, where the bullet travels through a short, parallel section of chamber in a straight line without spin before hitting the rifling.

THE CARTRIDGE CASE AND CHAMBER

The function of the cartridge case is to contain all the necessary parts that make up the self-contained metallic cartridge and provide a breech seal upon firing. Headspace, the dimensional fit of the cartridge in the chamber, and the distance the bullet sits from the start of the rifling, all have an effect upon performance. Firstly let us consider headspace, which is the distance between the breech face to that part of the chamber which stops the forward movement of the cartridge case. As a simple measurement it is the small gap between the head of a headspace gauge or cartridge, and the bolt or breech-block face.

There are four ways of obtaining headspace: the rimless case that sits against a shoulder; rimmed and belted (a form of forward rim), which gives headspace against the rim and belt respectively; and the rimless straight taper case that sits against the mouth of the case. The majority of the latter are low pressure pistol cartridges, which, for most UK shooters, are no longer relevant.

One thing to bear in mind is that whatever the design for headspacing, there is always clearance between the cartridge and the chamber to make efficient loading possible. With commercial cartridges there are also manufacturing tolerances, so it is possible to finish up with two extremes – for example the cartridge on minimum tolerance and the chamber on maximum, or vice versa – and even though it may be just a few thousandths of an inch, when it comes to deter-

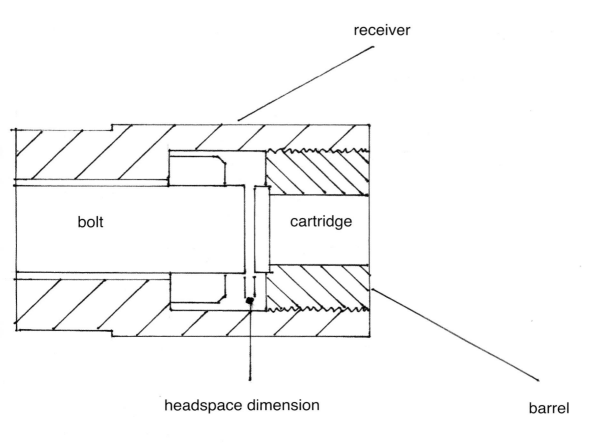

Headspace drawing based on bolt action
and rimmed cartridge

Headspace is the dimension between the head of the cartridge and the bolt face.

mining the very best ballistic performance these
can be matters of influence.

Experiment

The following experiment was to observe the
effects of increasing headspace in relationship to
both accuracy and the effects on the cartridge case.

Equipment

A Parker Hale 7.62mm T4 bolt-action rifle with
extra bolt heads modified to give
0.005/0.010/0.015 and 0.020in excess headspace; ammunition: hand-loaded Norma cases
with 168-grain Speer Gold Match bullets; MEN
commercial 7.62 NATO ammunition.

One of the signs of excess headspace can be (but is not always) a protruding primer after firing.

Modified bolt heads reduced in length on the workshop grinder to give different amounts of headspace, demonstrating the convenience of the detachable bolt head design.

Results

Tests were carried out at fifty yards (46m) with a large backing sheet behind the target in the expectancy that some shots might 'go a bit wild' – though this turned out not to be the case. Some fliers were experienced up to 2in (5cm) away from the rest of the group, and with 0.005in excess headspace a punctured primer occurred. At 0.020in excess headspace (the maximum for safety reasons) accuracy was very good, as good as when correctly headspaced.

The best group was achieved with the hand-loaded ammunition, with two bullets almost through the same hole and the third within half an inch. Grouping might have been improved further with a change of riflescope, the one in use being fitted with a post reticule which can, without great care in use, result in slight errors in elevation. Re-testing gave the same sort of good grouping.

All the fired cartridge cases on examination bore no signs of what is regarded as a classic case of excess headspace, the protuberant primer. At 0.020in excess headspace the hand-loads, which may be regarded as a fairly 'soft' load, had carbon deposits on the neck and shoulder, and traces in lines down the full length of the body. The MEN commercial ammunition showed no signs of a leakage of gases.

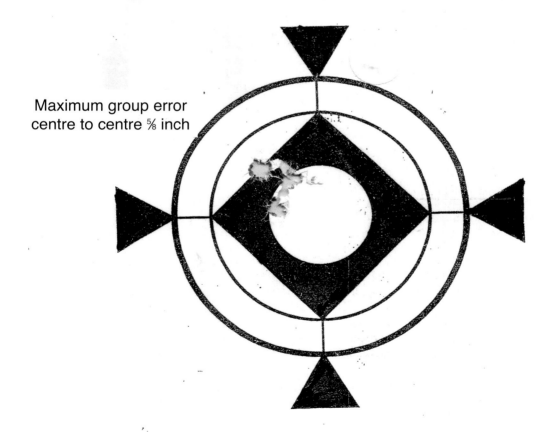

Maximum group error centre to centre ⅝ inch

Three-shot group produced with zero headspace.

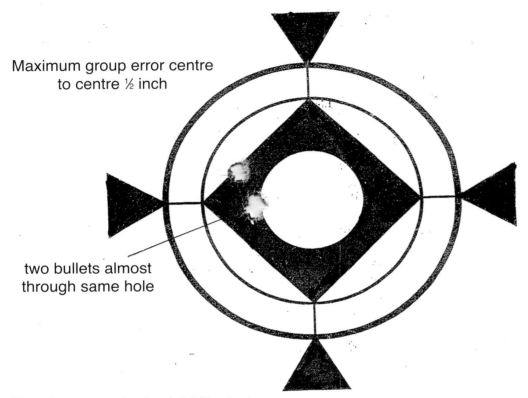

Maximum group error centre to centre ½ inch

two bullets almost through same hole

Three-shot group produced with 0.020in headspace.

All the primers, whatever the excess headspace dimension, were flattened more than those with the correct headspace. As the headspace increased, bruising of the primer around the firing pin strike increased until it was very visible with the naked eye, especially with the MEN ammunition.

Comparing the hand-loaded fired cartridge cases with the MEN cases showed a shorter neck on the hand-loaded, although the dimensions when loaded were almost identical. The MEN cartridge cases had lengthened 0.006in more than the hand-loaded cases.

Conclusion

Excess headspace introduces an unknown factor that may make accuracy more sensitive to the load as well as being potentially unsafe and reducing cartridge case life. The good results with 0.020in excess headspace cannot be explained – it is just a fact. The carbon deposits along the cartridge case of the 'softer' hand-loaded ammunition, along with the short re-formed neck, suggest the case may have moved back a tiny amount in the chamber before fully sealing, and then the case stretching at the head to come up against the bolt face.

The commercial MEN ammunition showed good sealing at the neck and shoulder with considerable impact upon the primer, indicating sealing from the front of the cartridge case and stretching in front of the case head. This appears to be borne out after measuring the fired cases, when it was found the MEN cases had stretched more than the Norma hand-loaded cases.

Cartridge cases before and after firing: MEN commercial on the left, with a longer neck after firing than the hand-load on the right. The flattened primer on the left of the hand-load was fired with 0.005in excess headspace.

Note: Tests are only valid for this rifle with the loads used; a different rifle with other loads/makes of cartridge could well give different results.

RIMLESS VERSUS RIMMED CARTRIDGE CASE

The rimless cartridge case is very familiar because it has become the most common design and is especially useful when feeding from a magazine. By comparison the rimmed design is regarded by many as 'old hat', and apart from survivors of an earlier age, is very much on the wane. For its part, the belted case has its own niche as a specialist cartridge for more extreme use.

When fired, there is a subtle difference between rimless and rimmed/belted cartridges, although it is worth bearing in mind that what I am about to describe all takes place in less than 1/1000 of a second.

Due to manufacturing tolerances already described resulting in the comparatively sloppy fit of a rimless cartridge in the chamber, as the firing pin strikes the primer it is pushed forwards, until the shoulder of the case rests hard against the shoulder of the chamber. Only then can the firing pin punch into the primer to ignite the priming charge. There is considerable force from the primer ignition (usually sufficient to fire a bullet into the lead of the rifling even without a powder charge) and initially it tries to push the primer backwards, out of the primer pocket. Then as the main charge starts to burn and build up pressure, the cartridge case starts to expand sideways until it fills the chamber. When the neck, shoulder and walls of the case are forced against the chamber wall they form a perfect seal, but as a result cannot move back to take up the headspace gap. As a result the brass stretches often only a few thousandths of an inch in front of the head of the case until it moves back enough to contact the bolt or breech block, at the same time seating the primer back into its pocket.

With a rimmed cartridge, headspace is more controlled, as all we have to consider is one single dimension – the rim thickness. This also has

the advantage in some designs of the rim being completely captive when the breech is closed. Even with simpler (or more primitive) arrangements, the rim butts up against the breech end of the barrel with the bolt or breech block close behind limiting movement, regardless of any other dimensional tolerances. In simple terms, the cartridge case can form to follow the dimensions of the chamber, but if correctly headspaced and in a sufficiently strong action, there is virtually no backward stretching of the case.

The belted cartridge acts in a similar manner to the rimmed design and is a sort of hybrid, with the heavy head of a rimless case reinforced by the belt, although the case wall in front of the belt can be quite thin.

BULLET SEATING

Bullet seating, and the distance it sits from the start of the rifling, is always an interesting issue, and a matter where there are slightly different views. Manufacturers, for good practical reasons such as loading ammunition that will be used in a great variety of rifles (even allowing for CIP and SAAMI specifications), have bullets seated in the case so that they sit a little bit back from the start of the rifling, by a minimum of around 0.030in. As the powder starts to burn, this small gap allows the bullet to move forwards fairly unimpeded until it starts to engage the rifling: in other words, it gets off to what might be called a flying start. The result is that pressure build-up is, in comparative terms, quite smooth and steady.

When there is a very long lead, giving a similar effect to a bullet seated too deep in its case, the length of travel before the bullet engages the rifling allows the burning gases to expand more quickly than with a shorter seating depth. The result is that pressures tend to be slightly lower, resulting in reduced velocity.

A favourite of hand loaders is the bullet seated in the case so that when chambered it is just in contact with the rifling, usually referred to as 'just kissing the rifling'. Such a set-up must, of course, be specific to one rifle and bullet shape: chambering such ammunition in another

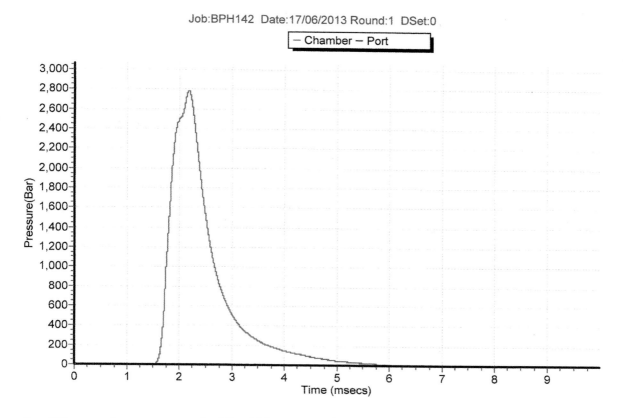

Job:BPH142 Date:17/06/2013 Round:1 DSet:0

— Chamber — Port

Proof House results testing service load for .223 Remington load (part 1).

rifle could cause problems, such as the bullet jammed hard into the rifling when the breech is closed, resulting in very high pressures when fired. It is not completely unknown in this sort of instance when the shot is not taken, upon opening the bolt it is found to be stiff, and the cartridge case pulled off the bullet, which is left jammed in the start of the rifling.

The idea of having the bullet 'just kissing the rifling' is as an aid to get it sitting concentric to the axis of the bore, although if there is any neck eccentricity the effect may not be as beneficial as expected. However, it is true that many rifles do deliver their best groups when the bullets are seated like this; the drawback is a steeper pressure curve, which often, though not always, means higher breech pressure.

What happens is that the bullet does not have the 'run-in' that it does when it is set back from the rifling. While the pressure is low it does not move, and therefore it takes increasing pressure to force it into the rifling. Also, the expanding gases from the burning powder effectively have less space to expand at this time in their burn (remember, in the standard method the bullet is already moving forwards); as a result pressure rise is rapid, potentially excessive, then, while velocity increases, results on the target may not reach expectations. The answer to overcoming these potential pressure problems is usually to slightly reduce the powder load to achieve normal working pressure, and following on from that, the result is quite often enhanced accuracy.

That is not the whole story, however, as this method of bullet seating as an aid to accuracy may only have a beneficial effect when the start of the rifling is even and clean cut – in other words, virtually as new. Once erosion caused by the hot gases starts to have an effect, it not only produces an uneven start to the rifling, but moves the contact point further from the bullet, and at the same time – as previously noted –

The British Proof Laboratory

Tel. 0121 643 3860   Fax. 0121 643 7872
www.gunproof.com   info@gunproof.com

London Proof House   Birmingham Proof House

Test Reference Number:	BPH142	**Date/Time Fired:**	17/06/2013 09:36:44
DataSet Number:	0		

Report For:	-	**Make:**	-
Calibre:	223 Rem	**Lot No:**	-
Case Type:	-	**C.O.L:**	56.55mm Average
Primer:	-	**Projectile Wt (gms):**	4.99
Charge:	-	**Max Avg Pressure:**	4300 bar
Proj Type:	77gr BTHP	**Incident Report No:**	N/A

Shot No	Velocity(2.5) (m/s)	Energy (Joules)	P1 (bar)
1	813.14	1649.69	2858.64
2	812.22	1645.95	2836.67
3	812.22	1645.95	2856.45
4	810.37	1638.47	2814.70
5	809.98	1636.89	2843.26
6	806.19	1621.61	2781.74
7	812.35	1646.48	2878.42
8	813.40	1650.74	2904.79
9	806.58	1623.18	2810.30
10	812.74	1648.06	2876.22
11	814.60	1655.61	2880.62
12	810.37	1638.47	2865.23
13	805.15	1617.43	2799.32
14	814.46	1655.05	2917.97
15	808.15	1629.50	2838.87

Summary Table

	Velocity	Energy	P1
Mean	810.79	1640.21	2850.88
Std Dev	3.04	12.28	38.53
Maximum	814.60	1655.61	2917.97
Minimum	805.15	1617.43	2781.74
Max-Min	9.45	38.18	136.23

Statistical Analysis   **No of Shots:** 15   **K1.n:** 3.52   **CIP Conformity**

Pn<=Ptmax   2851<=4300bar   Conforms
Pn+(K1n x Sn)<=1.15 Ptmax   2987<=4945bar   Conforms

The Birmingham Gun Barrel Proof House

Proof House results testing service load for .223 Remington load (part 2).

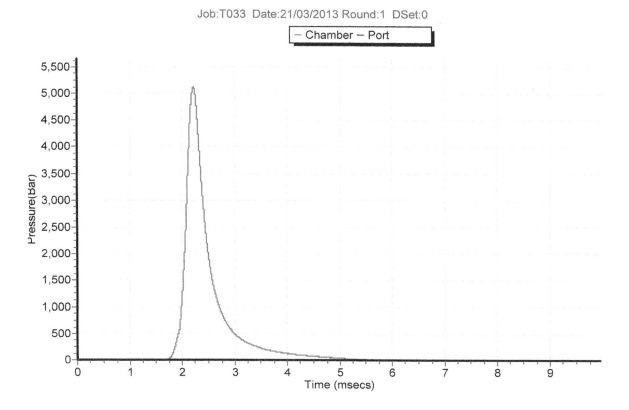

Job:T033 Date:21/03/2013 Round:1 DSet:0

— Chamber — Port

Proof House results testing proof load for .308 Winchester (part 1).

alters the pressure curve, hence affecting the velocity. Both factors may be seen as a change in accuracy.

Seating the bullet further forward may help restore some of the previous performance, but it is unlikely to be fully restored until the lead is re-cut with a throating reamer.

One of the reasons sometimes given for having the bullet in light contact with rifling is when bullets with a secant ogive are used. With the alternative tangent ogive, the transition between the ogive and the bearing surface is quite smooth and provides an inherent degree of self-alignment. The slightly more abrupt shape where the secant ogive joins the bearing surface of the bullet, does not self-align so well as the tangent ogive; a feature which can also be exaggerated by faults in the cartridge case.

The secant ogive, when just in contact with the rifling, at least in theory, gives a better chance of correct bullet-to-bore alignment. The

hybrid ogive, when it comes to bullet-seating depth, has the virtues of the tangent ogive and is therefore less sensitive in this respect than the pure secant ogive.

Black Powder Rifles and Bullet Seating

Black powder, breech-loading rifles need the bullet set back from the start of the rifling unless the barrel is cleaned between each shot. Otherwise, over a succession of shots, powder fouling can build up to such an extent that it becomes increasingly difficult to load subsequent cartridges because the bullet pushes against the fouling – and on a hot day or with a hot barrel, this can become surprisingly hard and crusted.

The choice of bullet comes down to cast lubricated, and probably the best of these is the bore-riding type where the front section of the bullet is calibre size and rides on top of the

The British Proof Laboratory

Tel. 0121 643 3860   Fax. 0121 643 7872
www.gunproof.com   info@gunproof.com

London Proof House

Birmingham Proof House

Test Reference Number:	T033	Date/Time Fired:	21/03/2013 15:57:00
DataSet Number:	0		

Report For:	BPL	Make:	BPL
Calibre:	308 Win - **PROOF**	Lot No:	-
Case Type	-	C.O.L:	70.70mm Average
Primer:	-	Projectile Wt (gms):	9.46
Charge:	-	Min Proof Pressure:	5188 bar
Proj Type:	146gr BT FMJ	Incident Report No:	N/A

Shot No	Velocity(2.5) (m/s)	Energy (Joules)	P1 (bar)
1	918.61	3991.38	5258.67
2	917.26	3979.66	5171.63
3	915.08	3960.77	5140.75
4	915.75	3966.57	5132.32
5	919.79	4001.64	5230.59
6	915.25	3962.24	5166.02
7	921.32	4014.97	5272.71
8	917.94	3985.56	5233.40
9	917.94	3985.56	5269.90
10	917.77	3984.09	5281.13

Summary Table

	Velocity	Energy	P1
Mean	917.67	3983.24	5215.71
Std Dev	1.98	17.19	57.57
Maximum	921.32	4014.97	5281.13
Minimum	915.08	3960.77	5132.32
Max-Min	6.24	54.20	148.81

Statistical Analysis   No of Shots: 10   K3.n: 2.36   CIP Conformity

Pn>=1.25 Ptmax	5216>=5188bar	Conforms
Pn-(K3n x Sn)>=1.15 Ptmax	5080>=4772bar	Conforms
Pn+(K3n x Sn)<=1.4 Ptmax	5352<=5810bar	Conforms

The Birmingham Gun Barrel Proof House

Proof House results testing proof load for .308 Winchester (part 2).

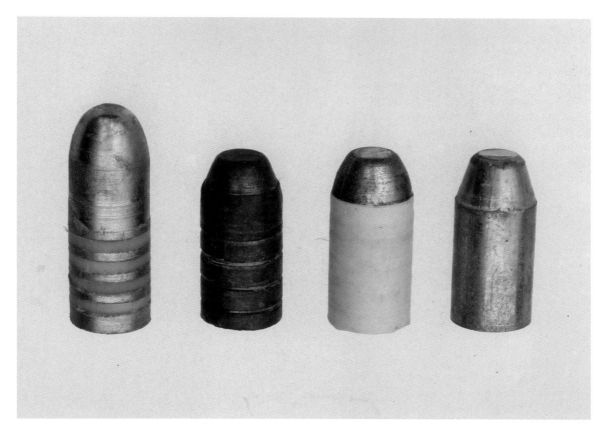

Bullets for breech-loading rifles. From left: bore-riding type with raised driving bands and wide lubrication grooves; cast with narrow lubrication grooves, which singles this out as a bullet for use with smokeless powder; paper patched; swaged for paper patching.

rifling, while the rear section is banded with lubrication grooves and engages the rifling. It is worth noting that lubrication grooves on bullets intended for black powder are wider than those intended for use with smokeless powder. The other option is paper-patched bullets, the original form of jacket on a bullet.

The lead in black powder rifles is usually longer and at a shallower angle than for smokeless powder. Unfortunately, modern reproduction rifles can be found where the manufacturer appears to have used chamber reamers with a comparatively short lead intended for smokeless powder and copper jacket bullets; however, these can be altered with a throating reamer.

The advantage of the long lead is that at a shallow angle the powder fouling does not have quite such a dramatic affect as it does in a steeper-angled lead. However, the real advantage is when paper-patched bullets are used, as the shallow-angled lead tends to compress the paper patch until it engages the rifling, while a steep lead can result in a torn patch and a 'flyer' on the target.

Another way of seating a paper-patched bullet, especially where case capacity is limited and it is desirable to increase the load, is to form bullet and patch calibre size. As the bullet sits only a short distance into the case, care needs to be taken in handling – although for the usual target use, this is no real problem. The paper-patched, pure lead bullet being calibre size, is, when loaded, sitting in the rifling in front of the chamber and much of the lead. A pure lead paper-patched bullet and black powder propellant loaded this way would seem to defy logic, but it works surprisingly well as it 'bumps up' to fit the rifling, and very good accuracy can be obtained.

POSITION OF THE POWDER IN THE CARTRIDGE

Ideally, with smokeless powder, the charge will almost fill the cartridge case; this is then at its most efficient. As a bonus for the hand loader it prevents dangerously large charges being accidentally loaded. With the popular move towards fitting sound moderators on centre-fire rifles, some shooters have experimented with greatly reduced powder charges in an attempt to produce subsonic loads, and this may introduce problems.

Tests in the USA during the inter-war period showed that where there was room in the case for the powder to move about, it had an effect on bullet velocity, depending whether the bulk of the powder was against the primer, up against the base of the bullet, or distributed fairly evenly along the length of the case. The best velocities were recorded with the powder against the primer, the worst with it against the bullet, and powder distributed fairly evenly gave mid-range results. With velocities around 2,600ft/sec (792m/sec) the extreme variation was up to 60ft/sec (18m/sec).

The other possible scenario is that of insufficient powder lying along the length of the case, but just below the primer hole. The powder just might then, instead of producing a gradual burn (again, in relative terms), ignite almost all at once. The theory is that this could cause a sudden pressure surge, a little more like an explosion than a controlled burn, with potentially dangerous results.

High bulk powders are regarded as one way forward for reduced loads, but probably by far the best way is to use shorter, reduced-capacity cartridge cases, and heavy for calibre bullets matched to the correct rate of rifling twist. Unfortunately this then means a dedicated rifle, only really acceptable for specialist use.

With black powder breech loaders, life is somewhat easier. As long as the bullet and wadding, where used, sit against the powder, usually with a modest degree of compression, it all works without problems. Coarser or finer powders can be used to alter velocities while retaining the same powder load. Too much powder, or a powder that is exceptionally slow, will

Dummy of an experimental .30 calibre cartridge intended for subsonic use based around a 150-grain bullet and modified 32-20 Winchester cartridge case.

result in a lot of powder burning in front of the muzzle, giving, in poor light, some impressive flames but reduced performance relative to the powder charge.

FEATURES OF THE RIFLE BARREL

There are four features of the rifle barrel that have an effect on ballistic performance and accuracy: the rifling, chamber dimensions, muzzle shape and barrel profile. The one we tend to take most note of is the rifling, not just the condition but the rate of twist, while form and number of grooves is often of secondary consideration. The chamber, one might think, is just a female form of the cartridge shape, a couple of thousandths or so of an inch bigger to allow the cartridges to enter, then to seal properly on firing – but it is actually a little more complicated than that.

As for the muzzle, the shape and finish at the end of the barrel and general condition are all important. The usual view on external barrel profile is the heavier the better for enhanced accuracy, but like so many things, apart from practical considerations of size and weight, this may be true some of the time, but not necessarily all of the time.

The Twist Rate of Rifling

The twist rate of rifling is commonly described as so many turns in a measured length, usually expressed in inches. For example, 1:12 means one complete turn of the rifling every 12in (30cm). This sort of measurement, which is easily understood, especially as a comparison between twist rates, was derived from the method of setting some types of early rifling machines.

There is an alternative method of measurement based on speed of twist relative to calibre. While the turn per inches is almost universal, the twist rate based on calibres has many uses, and does help to explain why larger calibre rifles usually have a slower twist rate than a much smaller one. For most purposes what we need to know is that the optimum twist rate is the slowest that will produce the desired accuracy, although a slightly faster twist may be necessary for practical reasons.

A good example of a twist rate giving more flexible performance is the 7.62 NATO rifle using a 1:12 twist that has to handle a number of different bullets including tracer, all of which it does very effectively. However, target shooters using this cartridge found that a 1:14 rate of twist was more desirable for target shooting using only the 147-grain military (ball) ammunition. A guide to determining the amount of spin necessary to stabilize a jacketed lead bullet can be arrived at by applying the Greenhill formula:

$$\text{Rifling twist} = \frac{150}{\text{length of bullet (in calibres}}$$

Note 1: This only applies to bullets having a specific gravity of around 10.9, although this formula gives reasonably close results for a lead bullet with a specific gravity of 11.35. Copper bullets and the like will have a different specific gravity, and the above formula will not hold true for them.

Note 2: Specific gravity is obtained by suspending a bullet and weighing it in air, then in water. The difference between the two weights is divided into the bullet weight and the resultant figure is the specific gravity.

Example 1: 7mm 120-grain flat-nosed bullet, 0.275in calibre, 0.887in long

Length in calibres $= \frac{0.885}{0.275} = 3.218$
Twist rate in calibres $= \frac{150}{3.218} = 46.613$ calibres
Therefore rifling twist rate in inches $= 46.613 \times 0.275 = 12.818$, nominally 1:13 twist

In practice we know that a 1:12 twist will stabilize this 120-grain bullet.

Example 2: 7mm 162-grain bullet 1.363in long, 0.275in calibre

Length in calibres $= \frac{1.363}{0.275} = 4.956$
Twist rate in calibres $= \frac{150}{4.956} = 30.266$ calibres
Therefore rifling twist rate in inches $= 30.266 \times 0.275 = 8.323$in. In practice this bullet will adequately stabilize using a 1:9 twist.

Applying this formula to a larger calibre lead bullet may not yield quite such good results but is still a useful indicator of the rifling twist rate required.

Example 3: A .450 calibre 500-grain round-nosed bore-riding lead bullet 1.320in long

Length in calibres $= \frac{1.320}{0.450} = 2.933$
Twist rate in calibres $= \frac{150}{2.933} = 51.142$ calibres
Therefore twist rate in inches $= 51.142 \times 0.450$
$= 23.013$in

In practice 1:22 is the practical minimum, 1:20 more the norm, while for long-range target shooting with these heavy bullets launched at subsonic velocities 1:18 works very well, nothing faster being required.

With any of these calculations the form and structure of the bullet can have an effect. A fairly blunt-nosed bullet with a long bearing surface may not require the same twist rate as, say, a lighter weight (for calibre) long-nosed spire-point bullet with a shorter bearing surface but similar overall length; also, something like a hollow point design has the centre of gravity further back than its length might suggest. This formula can therefore only ever be a guide, and we usually come back to obtaining stability with a number of different bullets by opting for a rifling twist rate that is slightly faster than perhaps calculated.

Speed of Rotation

If we take, for convenience, the example of a bullet leaving the barrel at 3,000ft (900m)/sec with a twist rate of 1:12, what is the rotational speed of the bullet? For the purposes of this calculation we can ignore the fact that the bullet will not actually travel 3,000 feet in one second, due to loss of velocity because of air resistance, but what is important is the initial velocity, and the speed of rotation actually wanes more slowly than forward velocity.

Therefore 1:12 twist = one turn per foot, so a bullet travelling 3,000 feet in one second means 3,000 revolutions in that time. However, rotational speed is normally measured in revolutions per minute (rpm), so $3,000 \times 60\text{sec} = 180,000\text{rpm}$.

At this sort of rotational speed it is apparent why accuracy of manufacture without any out-of-balance factors is of great importance.

The Chamber

Ideally the chamber should be of the minimum practical tolerance that allows it to accept all commercial ammunition, and formed without any ovality or lack of concentricity between the changes of form. Such errors may occur due to sloppy manufacturing techniques such as polishing the chamber after reaming, part reaming by hand, or reamer faults such as an undersized pilot allowing it to 'wobble' or, to put it in more precise terms, to rotate out of true with the axis of the bore.

Many such faults will leave the cartridge lying at a slight angle to the axis of the bore and with the head of the case out of square to the bolt or breech block. In the search for the very best ballistic performance these are generally regarded by accuracy enthusiasts as undesirable features. However, rifles can at times be odd things to deal with and sometimes the results are different to what is expected. Experience tells us that some rifles, standard-chambered to CIP or SAAMI specifications and using good commercial ammunition, will perform superbly as originally manufactured, and sometimes there will be little to be gained by what are seen as improvements. Most rifles, however, will be ballistically more efficient just by neck sizing and working up a load to suit, and will therefore perform better in the accuracy stakes.

The Lead

The lead I have already touched on in relationship to bullet seating depth, but again some matters are based around practical considerations rather than perfect theory. For example, a production rifle chambered for the 6.5 × 55mm Swedish cartridge will have a long lead to accommodate the long, blunt-nosed 159-grain bullets that might be used. Something like a 120-grain bullet even set out a long way in the neck is still well back from the start of the rifling, but with this cartridge accuracy is

A cutaway chamber is very useful for detecting cartridge fit, especially when developing a hybrid or wildcat cartridge.

still normally very good, although bullet skid may be increased.

Another theoretically imperfect matter is the rifling twist, which at 1:7½ to stabilize the 159-grain bullet is much faster than is needed for the 120-grain bullet, which could exaggerate imperfections in the bullet, but again seems to have little real adverse effect.

I have included this to make the point that what happens in practice can sometimes defy what we might expect in theory. Having said that, it is most likely that a 6.5 × 55mm Swedish produced with a lead and twist rate to suit the shorter, lighter bullet would outperform a standard rifle, but whether the gain in performance would be sufficient to justify the investment or be of real benefit for its intended use is a different matter.

The Rifle Muzzle

The rifle muzzle can be a relatively neglected area, and while shooters can get excited about throat erosion, that section of rifling that is last in contact with the bullet is actually of equal, if not greater (depending upon the degree of damage) importance.

Crowning is found in four types: flat, rounded, flat-recessed and eleven-degree. The simple flat finish machined square to the axis of the bore is still found on some old rifles, and while looking a little odd to modern eyes, works very well: the disadvantage is the potential for accidental damage. The rounded form is common on sporting rifles, partly for its streamlined looks, and actually forms a sort of recessed crown but with a tapered end to the rifling. Flat-recessed originated on target rifles but is finding

An extreme example of a neglected rifle muzzle. The corrosion is the result of leaving a sound moderator in place instead of removing and cleaning it.

favour with sporting rifle users seeking that extra little bit of accuracy; it is effectively the same as flat crowning, but being formed in a recess achieves better protection from possible damage to the end of the rifling. The shallow eleven-degree crowning developed around bench-rest shooting. However, working with a variety of calibres and cartridges, I have never found this has any advantage over the square-recessed type.

Once muzzle erosion occurs, which, with use, is inevitable, it is not necessarily evenly distributed around the end of the rifling. As the bullet just leaves the muzzle, high velocity and therefore high pressure gases squirt out unevenly, with a tendency to tip the bullet when there is more gas escape one side than another. These gases overtaking the bullet contribute towards inaccuracy by enhancing bullet yaw (see Chapter 3). The old-timers I knew would often, as a matter of course, chop about 1¼in (3cm) from the end of a part-worn barrel, then recrown it in an attempt to improve accuracy, and usually this was beneficial.

Barrel Profile

The barrel profile is important, especially when consistent accuracy is required over a number of shots. When a rifle is fired and the bullet accelerates up the barrel, it sets up vibration and imparts a whipping motion to the barrel which is normally referred to under the 'catch-all' name of 'barrel harmonics'. A lightweight barrel is less stiff than a heavyweight barrel, so the amplitude of the vibration is greater and affects it more than a heavy profile barrel.

Besides using a heavier barrel, another way to reduce vibration frequency is to thicken the muzzle end of the barrel or fix a weight to it, like a sound moderator. In reality, for most sporting purposes as long as this effect is consistent and the bullet leaves the barrel at the same point of the vibration sequence, then accuracy is hardly impaired. Another advantage to the target shooter is that a heavy barrel means a bigger heat sink to help absorb the heat generated by firing.

However, a barrel only needs to be sized relative to the cartridge: in other words, suitable to cope with the amount of energy produced. For example, something like a medium Mauser profile is quite adequate to act as a heavy barrel when chambered for a cartridge such as the .22 PPC. If the same barrel were .30 calibre and chambered for the 30-06 Springfield cartridge, it would only rate as a medium sporter barrel due to the bigger calibre, reduced wall thickness and more energy produced driving a heavier bullet. To get the same effect as the .22 PPC with the medium Mauser profile barrel the 30-06 would have to opt for a much heavier so-called bull barrel.

The barrel profile, regardless of the weight of barrel, is also important. Some of the early smokeless powder breech-loading barrel shapes have a large radius sweeping up to a short nock form, with the rest of the barrel slim and almost parallel, and these rarely perform as well as later shapes. Most of these are not only more substantial, but the nock form in front of the receiver is several inches long, followed by a long curved section running into a straight taper for the rest of the barrel.

Not so attractive in appearance is a short parallel followed by a straight taper to the muzzle, as found on some heavy bench-rest competition barrels, but it is also one way of making a reasonably rigid lightweight barrel in a slim form. The other way to often improve performance, meaning to make it more rigid and less prone to vibration, is to shorten it, but this is anathema to those seeking maximum velocities.

Whatever is tried, including fluted barrels, we have to live with the fact that the barrel becomes almost alive when fired, and different weights, profiles, chambering and cartridge loads all have an influence; it can therefore simply come down to a matter of finding the best practical compromise. Quality and consistency of manufacture is always important, and any error, such as the outside of the barrel being eccentric to the bore, is a recipe for poor accuracy, especially as the barrel starts to heat up: if a barrel wall is thicker on one side than the other, it will start to bend in a similar manner to a bimetal strip. Even the popular and visually attractive fluting on barrels, if not carried out with the greatest care, can introduce inaccuracy that was not apparent with the barrel in its original round, concentric form.

THE EFFECT OF FITTING SOUND MODERATORS

For some years it was believed, and vigorously promoted by some of those opposed to the use of sound moderators on centre-fire rifles, that both accuracy and velocity were adversely affected by the fitting of a sound moderator. There was also the argument that they did not work because the sonic crack of the bullet in flight could not be masked – which is true, but ignores the fact that the reduction in muzzle blast was still beneficial, especially to the user. Also the sound is different depending upon the position from where it is heard, which can vary from a sort of 'scream' (usually what the user hears), to a 'whoosh' at a distance, or just a crack when at right-angles to the bullet's flight and at some distance down-range.

Shooting rabbits on a bank with a sound-moderated .22 rimfire magnum showed that if the closest animals were taken first, the others took little notice because the muzzle blast was negligible, and of course, the sound of the bullet in flight stopped before it reached the rabbits further up the bank. Strangely, the sound (thump) of the bullet's strike on flesh did not seem to alarm them too much, but a miss, where earth was thrown up, would send them scuttling away.

Velocity, it was at one time believed, was reduced because, with a sound moderator fitted, the point of impact of the bullet was usually lower, but this was due to the effect of fitting a weight (the sound moderator) to the end of the barrel rather than any reduction in velocity. Also that weight to the end of the barrel, as already noted, alters the vibration pattern, usually in a manner beneficial to accuracy.

Tests I carried out when this debate was on-going in the early 1990s proved that, with both .22 rimfire rifles and centre-fire rifles (in this case .223 Remington, 6.5 × 55mm Swedish, and 7.62mm NATO) fitted with a properly designed and fitted sound moderator, there was no detrimental effect on either velocity or accuracy. In fact the results indicated just the opposite, where bullets exiting through a sound moderator suffered less from variations in muzzle velocity as compared to a rifle without one.

Over ten shots the sound-moderated rifle would sometimes record a slightly higher average velocity. Consistent velocities are, of course, one important element when striving for good groups, although this on its own is not necessarily a guarantee of good accuracy.

Regarding accuracy, this was usually improved (partly due to the above) with a properly fitted sound moderator with adequate clearance in the baffles so they do not in any way interfere with the passage of the bullet. When erosion sets in and the central hole through the baffles is no longer truly round, then accuracy can be impaired due to different volumes of gas escaping on either side of the bullet.

There can be an improvement in accuracy related to the user. The lack of muzzle blast and reduction in recoil (the gases hitting baffles act in a way similar to a muzzle brake) make a rifle much more comfortable to shoot, and this allows the shooter to concentrate better on taking the shot, and the enhanced confidence usually results in less tendency to flinch. The down side for some types of field sports is a muzzle-heavy, unbalanced rifle, and the tendency then is to attach further 'accuracy aids' such as bipods to make the rifle more manageable.

One area of confusion that arose in the days before sound moderators became an almost 'must have' accessory was linked to what are often called 'fully (sound) moderated' rifles. These have a gas bleed system, or series of holes drilled through the barrel wall to vent propellant gases into an expansion chamber positioned before the baffled area, so as to reduce bullet velocity. The usual intention is to reduce the velocity below around 1,050ft/sec (320m/sec) (air density will make a difference), making it subsonic and eliminating the sonic 'crack' of the bullet's flight. However, for sporting use where, for many types of quarry, there is a legal muzzle energy limit, the loss of velocity from this type of sound moderator would, in most cases, cause a drop in muzzle energy below the legal limit.

Note: There is a safety matter linked to this design of sound moderator, in that the holes drilled to vent some of the propellant gases into the expansion chamber need to be at a point where the powder burn is complete, otherwise

Sako rifle with prototype Mk II TLD sound moderator used for centrefire velocity testing.

unburned kernels of powder can accumulate in the expansion chamber with the potential for igniting it with a later shot.

Experiment

This experiment tested velocity with .22 rimfire and .308 Winchester ammunition to determine the differences between rifles with and without sound moderators.

Equipment

(a) BSA Martini .22 r/f rifle modified to sporter with 19in barrel and Parker Hale sound moderator; ammunition – Remington Thunderbolt HV and Eley Tenex (subsonic target grade)

(b) Sako .308 Winchester rifle with 22in barrel and Thomas Lowe Defence prototype MK II over-barrel sound moderator; ammunition – hand-loaded Norma cases with 168-grain Speer Gold Match bullets; chronograph – Pro-Tach by Competition Electronics Inc.

Results

The results recorded an average muzzle velocity over five shots:

.22 r/f without the sound moderator:
Eley subsonic 1,026.60ft/sec (312.9m/sec)
Remington supersonic 1,264.00ft/sec (385.27m/sec)

.22 r/f with the sound moderator fitted:
Eley subsonic 1,026.75ft/sec (312.95m/sec)

Remington supersonic 1,249.60ft/sec
(380.88m/sec)
Rimfire
Velocity spread without the sound moderator:
Eley subsonic 23ft/sec (7m/sec)
Remington supersonic 45ft/sec (13.7m/sec)

Velocity spread with the sound moderator fitted:
Eley subsonic 7ft/sec (2m/sec)
Remington supersonic 37ft/sec (11m/sec)
Centrefire
.308 Winchester without sound moderator
– 2,510ft/sec (765m/sec)
.308 Winchester with sound moderator fitted – 2,513ft/sec (766m/sec)
Velocity spread without the sound moderator – 12ft/sec (3.7m/sec)
Velocity spread with sound moderator fitted – 3ft/sec (90cm/sec)

Accuracy: As can be seen from the comparative tests with and without a bipod fitted (see Chapter 4), accuracy is usually unaffected and may, for several reasons, be enhanced.

Conclusion

With a sound moderator system comprising an expansion chamber and baffle section (that does not bleed off gases prior to the muzzle) velocities differ but to no great extent. Much depends upon the ammunition used and the velocity spread. With ammunition producing fairly consistent bullet velocities, the difference between sound-moderated and unmoderated is usually very small, with sometimes the sound-moderated rifle recording slightly higher average velocities (this follows the pattern of results recorded in the early 1990s: in those tests RWS .22 r/f HV recorded slightly higher average velocities with the sound moderator fitted).

Note: These brief tests are a guide, valid only on the day tested. Retesting will give similar but not necessarily the same results.

BARREL WEAR

Barrel wear is detrimental to matters such as velocity and accuracy, although one occasionally comes across visibly worn barrels that give far better accuracy than might be expected, and often it is not clear why this should be. There are several matters that influence barrel wear, to a very small extent the friction from the passage of the bullet, and, to a far greater extent, the erosive effect of the propellant gases at high pressure and the temperatures produced. Some cartridges, such as the low pressure 30-30 Winchester, have a good reputation for long barrel life, while, say, the 22-250 Remington, operating at much higher pressure and velocity, has earned a perhaps not entirely deserved reputation as a 'bit of a barrel burner' – meaning the barrel has a comparatively shorter accurate life due to accelerated wear.

With a rise in breech pressure there is also a rise in temperature, although this is not proportional, as temperature rises more quickly than a given increase in powder charge weight might at first suggest. Then within any pressure band there is the ratio of powder charge to calibre, particularly significant with bottleneck cartridge cases. Basically this means that burning more powder to improve performance also increases wear, and with a large cartridge case and small calibre, the heat and erosive effect of the propellant gases is concentrated on a smaller area than a similar design of cartridge but of larger calibre.

A further contributory factor is the rate of burn of the powder charge. If, to get increased performance but to keep within acceptable (service) breech pressures, a larger charge of slower burning powder is used, then more of the barrel bore is exposed to the main erosive effect of the propellant gases, as peak pressure will be at a point slightly further forward.

The peak degree of wear, as most shooters know, occurs at the throat in an area usually referred to as the turbulence point, which is influenced by cartridge case design. Take, for example, something like the .303 British, which has a shallow tapered cartridge case and small rounded shoulder, meaning the transition from chamber to barrel is comparatively smooth. The

turbulence point

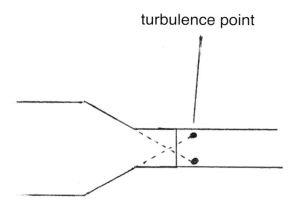

Shallow shoulder angle and short neck means the point of turbulence is in the lead of the barrel.

turbulence point

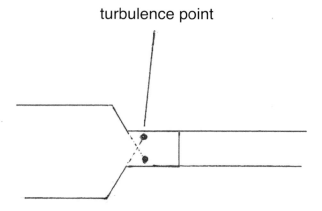

Steep shoulder angle and long neck means the point of turbulence is in the neck of the cartridge case.

The peak turbulence point with the shallower-angled shoulder and short neck occurs in the lead of the rifling. With a steeper-angled shoulder and long neck the peak turbulence point occurs inside the neck.

.404 Jeffrey with its long, tapered, 'Victorian' shoulder is another, and, like the .303, designed for ease of extraction and comparatively low breech pressures, all contributing to reduced turbulence of the propellant gases. Compare those with our 22-250 Remington with its fairly fat case, steep shoulder angle, small calibre and higher service pressure, and it becomes fairly obvious why turbulence of the propellant gases will be increased.

Yet there is also the theory that, if the turbulence point can be contained within the neck of the cartridge case by having a very steep shoulder, then it is better, from the point of reduced wear, than having it further forward in the barrel. So something like a .22 PPC, with its short, fat cartridge case, steep shoulder angle and long neck, gains in reducing barrel wear by containing the peak turbulence point within the neck of the cartridge case. It also operates at fairly high pressure, but because the powder charges are fairly small – in other words, the ratio of powder charges to calibre is fairly low – the overall result is usually a reasonably long, accurate barrel life.

As for that perennial question, 'What is the life of a barrel?', try looking at it in a different way: the time it is actually in use. After all, the life expectancy of most things is measured in time. As a simple example, if we take as a 'guesstimate' the accurate life of a sporting rifle barrel as 3,000 shots, and the time for a bullet to travel up the barrel as 1/1000 second, then in this instance:

Accurate barrel life $= 3,000 \times \frac{1}{1,000}$
$= 3$ seconds

When you have spent several hundred pounds rebarrelling a rifle, looked at from this perspective it does not seem to be much of a bargain, although in reality it is, of course, the number of shots that is important. What you cannot do is predict exactly, for any particular barrel, how many shots it will take until accuracy begins to suffer.

OPPOSITE: *Cartridge case designs with markedly different shoulders. From left: .22PPC; 22-250 Remington; .303 British; .404 Jeffrey.*

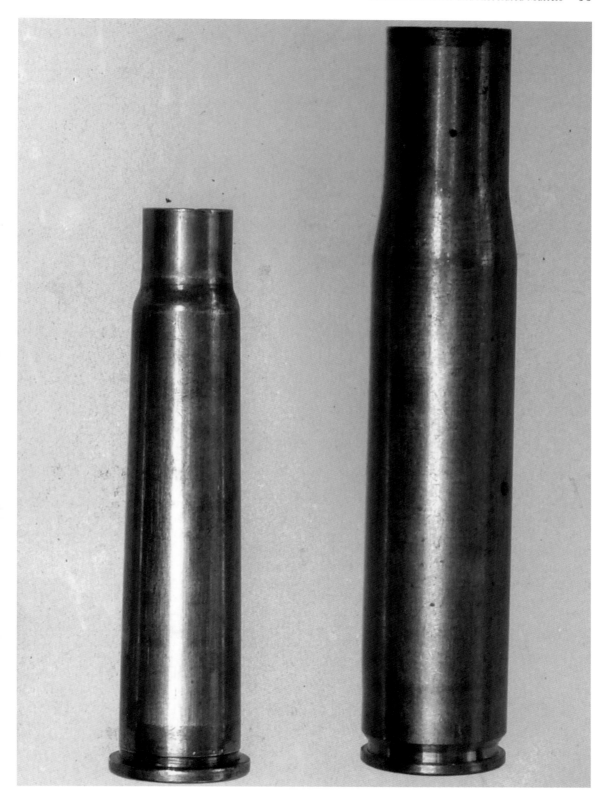

Chapter 3
External Ballistics and Associated Matters

External ballistics is, to most shooters, the really fascinating part of this subject; that being the bullet's flight covering the period of time and the distance travelled between it leaving the barrel and hitting the target. When any group of keen rifle enthusiasts is gathered together discussions often turn to matters relating to the bullet's flight, such as velocity, bullet weights and shapes. Yet expressions such as 'hyper-velocities', 'ballistic coefficients' and 'wind-bucking bullets' sometimes seem designed primarily to confuse the listener new to the subject.

All too often one can be left with the impression that once the subject is fully understood there is such scientific certainty to calculating the bullet's flight that doing all the right things will guarantee hitting the bull every time. However, I would advise anyone who has convinced themselves that the world of external ballistics is completely predictable to take the opportunity, if it arises, of watching tracer bullets go down range. They look strangely lazy in flight, often curling and winding their way before appearing to plunge downwards to strike the target – and suddenly everything seems to be not quite so certain, especially when ungovernable matters, such as nature's contrary winds, are added into this scenario.

BALLISTIC COEFFICIENT (BC) AND SECTIONAL DENSITY (SD)

If we look at the bullet just as a high-speed projectile, it is obvious that it needs to be streamlined for the best in-flight performance, but other needs may require designs where exceptional terminal performance overrides the requirement for the very best flight characteristics. Also, for aficionados of black powder rifles, fairly blunt-nosed, heavy bullets, launched at subsonic velocities, can perform very well, even at long range.

However, the faster a bullet is pushed, the more the shape is important, and the value quoted to indicate a bullet's ability to overcome air resistance is ballistic coefficient (BC). For those of a technical bent, this is the ratio of bullet weight to the square of its diameter and its form factor. Of these three parts, weight is important, because a heavy bullet retains energy better than a light one and this helps it push through the air. Energy is expressed in foot/pounds using the following formula:

$$\text{energy (ft/lb)} = \frac{m \times v^2}{450240} \quad \begin{array}{l} \text{[m = bullet weight in grains]} \\ \text{[v = velocity in feet per sec]} \end{array}$$

As for cross-sectional area, the smaller the diameter, the less the resistance as compared to a bigger, bulkier projectile. This ratio of weight to the square of a bullet's diameter is known as sectional density (SD), and not only is this ballistically important, but in live game shooting it has a considerable effect on penetration as part of its terminal performance. Good sectional density is one of the requirements for deep penetration.

'Form factor' means how streamlined – or in some cases, unstreamlined – a bullet is compared to an industry-standard projectile shape. What it means is that a pointed bullet almost always has a better ballistic coefficient than a blunter one, although in overall performance there are many factors that come into play, such as shape and length of ogive (radius in calibres), overall length and bullet weight, and shape at the heel, for example whether it has a flat base or a boat tail. Fortunately we do not have to worry

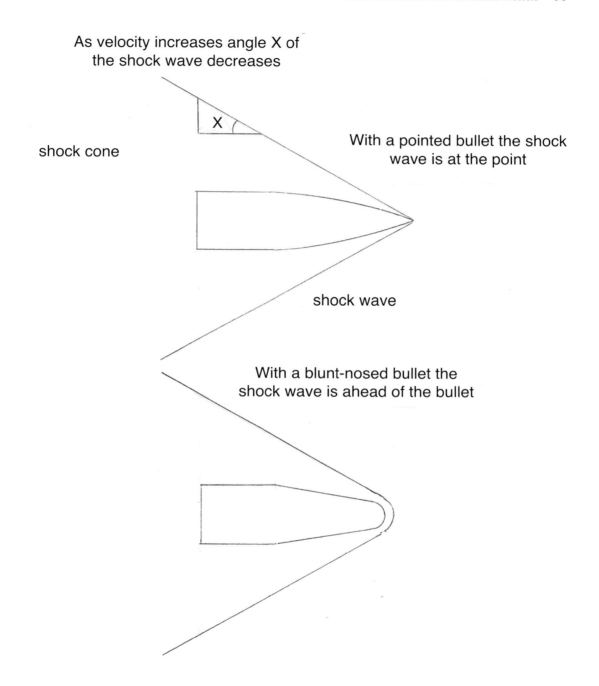

The supersonic bullet: with a pointed bullet the shock wave is at the point, with a round-nosed bullet the shock wave is in front.

about such minutiae, as each bullet/cartridge manufacturer supplies tables of ballistic coefficients which, if not perhaps always absolutely accurate, are sufficient for our purposes. The thing to remember is that the higher the figure quoted, the better the ballistic coefficient.

Take, for example, two .30 calibre spire-point bullets, one of 130 grains weight, the other 165 grains, almost identical in form but the heavier bullet having a longer bearing surface. In this instance the ballistic coefficient of the lighter bullet is .292 and the heavier one .392, so the heavier bullet is ballistically more efficient, which will become noticeable as the distance to the target increases.

Then consider a blunt-nosed bullet of the same calibre and 165 grains weight. Due to its relatively unstreamlined form the ballistic coefficient drops to .204, which, in spite of its weight advantage, means that ballistically it is not as good as the pointed bullet of 130 grains. Therefore, while this blunt-nosed bullet is not going to be your first choice for long-range precision shooting, it could be a better bet, depending upon its actual construction, for use against something like a moose at the comparatively short range encountered in a forested area.

VELOCITY

There is a tendency to believe that the faster the speed of a bullet (expressed as muzzle velocity, MV), the more its performance is enhanced, but at risk of upsetting those self-confessed 'velocity freaks', I have to say this is not necessarily the case. The problem that so often arises is that for any given calibre the highest initial velocities are achieved with the lightest bullets, which, as we have previously touched upon, may not give the best overall performance.

Consider two of the popular 6mm (.243) bullets, one of 70 grains, the other 100 grains, with the same ogive, but the heavier and therefore longer bullet having a greater sectional density and better ballistic coefficient.

This shows that in this case the 30 per cent heavier bullet, launched at a muzzle velocity nearly 10 per cent lower than the lighter bullet, has almost caught up with the performance of the lighter bullet by the 200 yard (180m) mark; but from this point on the heavier and ballistically more efficient bullet starts to gain.

What we can learn from this is that, for some uses at short range, light bullets driven at high velocities can have an advantage, but as distance

70-grain bullet, BC .260, SD .169, 100 yard zero:

Range	Muzzle	100 yards	200 yards	500 yards
Velocity ft/sec	3,700	3,284	2,895	1,905
Drop inches	-1.5	0	-1.7	-38.2
Energy ft/lb	2,128	1,677	1,303	564

100-grain bullet, BC .376, SD .242, 100 yard zero:

Range	Muzzle	100 yards	200 yards	500 yards
Velocity ft/sec	3,400	3,123	2,859	2,150
Drop inches	-1.5	0	-2.1	-38.5
Energy ft/lb	2,568	2,166	1,815	1,027

increases a heavier bullet of similar form will give not only better long-range characteristics but enhanced overall performance. Where a heavier bullet with a better ballistic coefficient always gains is that it is less susceptible to being pushed off course by a side or crosswind.

There are, of course, always limits on how far this sort of comparison can be taken. Make a bullet very heavy for its calibre, then it also becomes extraordinarily long, and this requires a change to the rifling twist in order to ensure stability, something that has practical limitations (maximum 7× calibre). Not only that, but the extra weight and increased kinetic friction (the resistance of accelerating it through the barrel) will mean reduced velocity to keep pressures within service limits. This then brings us to the rifle user's great bugbear, trajectory.

TRAJECTORY

Trajectory is the flight path of the bullet in the vertical plane. At an early age, say as a youngster throwing a stone, we are aware that projectiles fall back to earth even if at that time we do not recognize quite why this happens. In the case of a bullet it is the same, a combination of slowing down in flight due to air resistance, and the effect of gravity pulling the bullet back to earth. While gravity on a small object is not particularly strong — after all, you overcame gravity quite easily when picking up this book — it is constant force. The effect, as every rifle user is aware, is to produce a curved flight path until the bullet eventually falls to earth, although for most sporting purposes it is, in reality, usually stopped intentionally by use of a bullet catcher

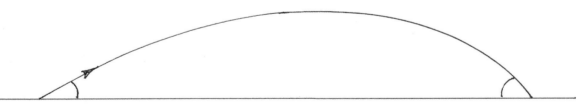

Maximum height of trajectory is
nearer point of impact than
the firing position

The angle of descent is greater than
the angle of departure

'Trajectory' is the bullet's flight path in the vertical plane.

or backstop prior to reaching its extreme range.

To allow for trajectory we have adjustable sights, but this does not alter the fundamental principle that at the longer distances the bullet will climb through the line of sight, fly above it for some distance, then drop into the line of sight again, which is normally the distance for which the rifle is zeroed. At very short range, and especially with a high-mounted riflescope, the first time the bullet intercepts the line of sight may be the zero point. Normally all this goes on unseen to the shooter, but at very long range and given the right atmospheric conditions, when using a high magnification spotting telescope, a sort of contrail (like sometimes seen at the tip of an aircraft wing) can be seen as the bullet approaches the target. This is most visible if there is a reasonable amount of windage, so the bullet curves in from one side of the line of sight.

As the distance to the target increases, the trajectory becomes correspondingly steeper. Even for the target shooter with the aid of ballistic tables and measured distances to target, it introduces an additional problem in that the bullet striking at a steep angle exaggerates any error in sighting in the vertical plane.

For the live game shooter shooting at longer distances – meaning, more often than not, the stalker out on the hill – there is a different set of problems to contend with, even ignoring for the moment all the other variables such as wind, visibility, angle of the beast to the shot, and so on. Normally 300 yards (275m) would be regarded as a long shot, which for a rifleman on the range is only a short distance on from the normal 200 yard (180m) zero. However, the target shooter knows exactly the distance the shot is being taken at, while for the stalker it is often a 'guesstimate'.

True, we now have available laser rangefinders, either separate hand-held ones, or built into the riflescope, but not everyone has one or maybe feels they can afford one. Also the tendency to use (for 'use' read 'come to rely on') technology can be a limiting factor, because when a shot has to be taken comparatively quickly there may be little time to spare to read off distances and adjust sights. The simple solution that most stalkers rely on is to learn to judge distances reasonably well, and to zero the rifle and sights at a range that will cover most eventualities likely to be encountered.

The kill area for a heart/lung shot is generally regarded as 4in (10cm) diameter, regardless of the size of the deer. While not a strictly accurate measurement, it is a useful guide and we get away with it even on smaller deer, which theoretically should require a more precise aim, because most of the cartridges used are actually far more powerful than are needed for these small animals.

Anyway, let us consider that stag out on the hill and a popular cartridge for this sort of sport, the .270 Winchester. One commercial load uses a 130-grain bullet and produces a claimed muzzle velocity of 3,140ft/sec (957m/sec), producing 2,840ft/lb (3,850 joules) muzzle energy. Manufacturers' claims for muzzle velocities are much more realistic than they were years ago, but we can be sure the stalker's rifle is very unlikely to exceed the quoted velocity. Depending upon matters such as barrel length and bore wear, the velocity could easily be less, so for the purposes of this exercise, we will round down the muzzle velocity to 3,100ft/sec (945m/sec).

The ballistic coefficient is unlikely to be of any great interest to the stalker, who is primarily interested in the end result, but we need it to find out the trajectory. At the same time we have to accept that a cartridge loaded with a soft-point bullet and fed from a magazine may be slightly deformed, thereby producing an imperfect streamlined shape – but that is an unknown factor, which, for most purposes, we have little choice but to ignore.

At this point it is worth noting that there is a story circulating on the internet, that misshapen exposed lead does not matter, because during its passage up the rifle barrel, the lead core becomes a molten mush and therefore the exposed lead at the nose changes shape or even melts: this story is not true. Another small matter to be aware of is that many ballistic tables, whether computer-based or hard copy, assume a line of sight 1½in (38mm) above the axis of the bore. With a riflescope where the objective lens is larger than 40mm diameter, or when there is a large ocular lens housing needing a high riflescope mount to clear a bolt handle, this measurement may well be greater, and so the line or trace of the trajectory would start off at a larger measurement than the standard minus 1½in.

.270, 130-grain bullet, MV = 3,100ft/sec (945m/sec), BC = .392 LOS over bore axis 1.5in

Using a ballistic programme and the 4in (10cm) vital zone – meaning no more than 2in above the line of sight and 2in below – we find that 'zero' needs to be at 222 yards (203m), giving a maximum range of 259 yards (237m). In other words, out to around 250 yards (229m) one can take aim and be fairly confident that no sort of aiming-off to compensate needs to be made, or indeed should really be considered, with live game shooting. To improve upon this performance and extend the range to around 300 yards (275m) would require a bullet with a better ballistic coefficient, an increase in velocity, or both.

Having become slightly disillusioned with our .270 Winchester (not really, just a turn of phrase), it could be worth turning to something a bit more powerful, such as a 7mm Remington magnum, in our search for the performance we feel is necessary but which can be difficult to achieve.

Take as an example this 7mm Remington magnum load:

7mm 140-grain bullet, MV = 3,150ft/sec (960m/sec), BC = .485

This increases the velocity slightly over the .270 Winchester and uses a bullet with a higher ballistic coefficient. Even with this load we find that to fall within the 4in (10cm) 'kill zone', and putting in a riflescope height over bore axis of 1.8in (4.6cm) – which can be an advantage for long range shooting – rather than 1.5in (3.8cm), the 200 yard (180m) zero is now equivalent to 234 yards (214m), and the kill zone range extended to 272 yards (249m): an improvement, but not by a great deal.

However, if, for practical purposes, we regard the kill zone on a big red stag as being of 6in diameter and re-zero for 270 yards (247m),

the bullet will strike at all distances out to 316 yards (289m) within the 6in (15cm) kill zone. All this really indicates is that it is actually rather difficult, with many cartridges commonly used for stalking, to zero at a suitable distance that might take us out to the 300 yard (274m) mark without aiming off or with sight adjustment. The answer for the sportsperson is simple: you stalk closer – that, after all, is the name of the game: stalking, not sniping!

Uphill and Downhill Shooting

Gravity has its most obvious effect on a body travelling in the horizontal plane, so if we alter the angle a bullet is fired, from the rifle muzzle to the point of impact the distance travelled will be different to that along the horizontal. This is not an unusual scenario when stalking or hunting in hilly country where occasionally very steep shots may be taken and allowance has to be made for the tendency to shoot high.

Consider a downhill shot at a depressed angle of thirty degrees using the .308 Winchester cartridge, a rifle zeroed for 200 yards (185m), riflescope height 1.5in (3.8cm), with a 150-grain spire-point bullet propelled at a muzzle velocity of 2,800ft/sec (853m/sec) and with a ballistic coefficient of .359. Reference to the diagram shows that our 200-yard zero is now actually extended to 227 yards (208m) as an angled shot.

However, in really difficult terrain a shot nearer sixty degrees to the horizontal is not completely unknown. I can vouch for this, having once hung over a dizzying drop to take a shot at a 'beastie' down below. Then a 200-yard (185m) shot translates to the equivalent of just about half that distance along the horizontal. This means the bullet will strike 2in (5cm) high, that being the height of the trajectory at 100 yards (90m) when zeroed at 200 yards.

The principle also applies to shooting upwards, as the gravitational force is constant across the horizontal distance covered, not an increasing force. Shooting really steeply downhill, though, could result in a tiny increase in velocity being aided slightly by gravity, which would contribute to an even higher bullet impact point.

EFFECT OF SHOOTING AT AN ANGLE

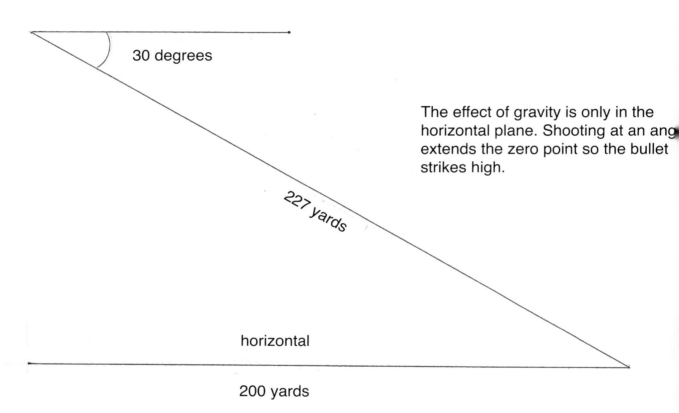

30 degrees

The effect of gravity is only in the horizontal plane. Shooting at an ang[le] extends the zero point so the bullet strikes high.

227 yards

horizontal

200 yards

Gravity is only exerted in the horizontal plane, so shooting at a downhill (or uphill) angle effectively moves the zero point forwards, giving a tendency to shoot high.

THE EFFECT OF WIND

Wind is very much the great unknown in its effect on a bullet's flight, due mainly to its variability. There are some basic rules: a side- or cross-wind will push the bullet sideways from its aimed line, a head-wind causes the bullet to strike a little low, while a tail-wind causes it to strike a little high. The greatest impact upon the bullet's flight is side-wind, and one has to consider the following:

* Wind is rarely constant
* A side-wind is not necessarily at ninety degrees to the bullet's line of flight, and the angle may vary along the line of flight
* The force of the wind can vary over the height of the bullet's trajectory
* The drag caused by a side-wind is greater than any effect caused by a head- or tail-wind

On a rifle range there are usually wind flags along the side of the range which provide an indication of what the wind is doing. However, having lain on the firing point of a range noted for its tricky wind and observed the 600 yard (550m) flag flying in one direction while the flag adjacent to the butts flew the opposite way, we can only conclude that experience in 'doping the wind' is one of the target rifle user's greatest attributes.

With live game shooting we have the advantage that most shots are taken at comparatively short distances, which minimizes the wind effect. On the debit side, there is no reliable indicator of how the wind is behaving. Devices to measure wind speed and direction are a help (if one has time to fiddle about with such things) but are only relevant at the point they are used. What we can do is learn from experience to judge the wind, and to do what we can to minimize its effect.

Compensating for Side-wind

The problem with side-wind, even at a fairly constant blow, is, as we have already noted, that it is very rarely at right angles to the bullet's line of flight, so guessing its actual effect becomes a little more difficult. The good news is that the shallower the angle, the less its effect, and when wind flags are in place a fair idea of its impact can be estimated using what is generally called the 'cross-wind component' that appears in some range score books. This is a simple calculation based on a factor of 1.00 for a side-wind at 90 degrees, with a reduction factor for some lesser angles. So a 12mph (19km/h) side-wind at three and nine o'clock is at 90 degrees and has its full value: $1 \times 12 = 12$mph

* At two, four, eight and ten o'clock the factor is 0.87, so with a 12mph wind the effect is reduced to $0.87 \times 12 = 10.44$mph (16.8km/h)
* At one, five, seven and eleven o'clock the factor is 0.50, so with a 12mph wind the effect is reduced to $0.50 \times 12 = 6$mph (9.65km/h)
* It is accepted that the factor for twelve and six o'clock is zero, as the effect on the bullet striking high or low is considerably less than sideways drift; but it is still worthy of note, especially at longer ranges and in high wind conditions

Method of Reducing the Side-wind Effect

I remember talking to a keen shooter who believed he had the answer to side-wind: 'I send the bullets out so fast,' he declared, 'that they get to the target so quick the wind does not have time to have any effect.' Well, there is partial truth in his theory, but it is not quite that simple. What he was doing, of course, to get very high velocities was use light bullets relative to the calibre and ignoring the other important matter affecting the bullet's flight that we have already looked at, the ballistic coefficient.

When it comes to side-wind there is a matter called lag time to consider, this being the difference between the bullet's theoretical flight time in a vacuum and that in air. A bullet at a muzzle velocity of, say, around 2,800ft/sec (532m/sec) would travel that distance in one second in a vacuum, but in reality due to air resistance, or more correctly, aerodynamic drag, it will take longer, depending upon the ballistic coefficient, nearer 1.5sec, to cover 2,800ft. Lag time is the difference between the theoretical and actual time of flight – in other words, it is simply a measurement of ballistic inefficiency. The longer a bullet takes to get to the target compared to its theoretical vacuum time, the greater the potential for wind drift. The way to reduce lag time is to use a bullet with a better ballistic coefficient, not necessarily a light bullet.

As ever, it becomes something of a balancing act, as increased velocity can reduce lag time, and a better ballistic coefficient will do the same, but this means a heavier bullet and therefore often reduced velocity. This is not as bad as it may at first seem, as the ballistic coefficient actually has a greater effect than velocity. This is why long-range target shooters favour heavy, very low drag (VLD) bullets. The theoretical (vacuum) flight time and actual flight time increase due to a reduced muzzle velocity (compared to a lighter bullet), but the lag time decreases due to the better ballistic coefficient. Look at it as simply a matter of aerodynamic efficiency – although sometimes, all is not quite what it at first seems.

Have you ever lain on the rifle range and wondered, on a blustery day, why the chap with the .223 Remington is not doing so well at 600 yards as the shooter next to him with an early .450 breech-loading black powder rifle? The .223, with something like a 50-grain pointed bullet, is probably producing nearly three times the muzzle velocity of a .450-500-grain blunt-nosed bullet, yet the old technology is having less trouble with the wind, even though it takes longer for the bullet to arrive at the target.

What we have to remember here once again is that lag time is the difference between theoretical vacuum flight time and actual flight time, not total elapsed flight time. Also, as weight is an important part of the ballistic coefficient, we find that the big, heavy, blunt-nosed bullet still has a ballistic coefficient of around .320 as compared to the .223s, being nearer .246. In other words, in practice it usually takes more wind to push a big, heavy, slower bullet off course than a lighter, faster one.

What Actually Happens?

It would be easy to assume that with a side-wind, especially one at 90 degrees, the bullet simply drifts bodily sideways in flight, a bit like a child's helium-filled balloon is pushed along in a garden breeze. However, the effect of side-wind is slightly more complex than that because we are dealing with a projectile that is comparatively long for its diameter and rotating at high speed about its axis.

For a bullet to be fully stable in flight means it flies point forward, rather than tumbling end over end or yawing badly from side to side. In the relatively rare condition of still air the bullet does fly point forward in a straight line – apart, of course, from its trajectory and a small matter called ballistic drift, which we will come to later. Add in a side-wind, and we know the bullet drifts off course relative to the strength and direction of the wind.

This happens because the bullet reacts rather like a church weathervane and tries to turn its head into the oncoming wind: by that I mean the wind generated by the bullet's high-speed passage through the air plus the cross-wind. What it means is the bullet is no longer pointing forward, but is flying with its axis at a very shallow angle, often less than one degree, to the line of sight. This causes an uneven aerodynamic drag, and while it may seem a bit odd, with a side-wind from the right the bullet's axis will turn slightly to the right (relative to the line of sight), but the drag causes it to drift left and vice versa.

Not a job to normally carry out on the rifle range, but there are a number of formulae to calculate wind deflection, the simplest being to multiply the side-wind factor by the lag time (if known) – which is a bit of fun for anyone keen enough to look into this in more depth without relying on ready-made ballistic tables.

So – drift = side-wind factor × lag time. An easy example would be to find the drift of a bullet at 1,000 yards with a muzzle velocity of 3,000ft/sec, a lag time of 0.5sec and a 15mph (24km/h) cross-wind at five o'clock. We have to take into account the side-wind compensation figure, which in this case is 0.5, as well as convert miles per hour to feet per second to get the deflection in feet and 1mph = 1,4667ft/sec.

Therefore drift $= \frac{15\text{(mph) x } 1.4667\text{ft/sec}}{0.5\text{ (compensation for side-wind)}}$
$\times 0.5$ (lag time)
$= \frac{22.0005}{0.5} \times 0.5$
$= 44.001 \times 0.5$
$= 22.005\text{ft} @ 1,000\text{yd}$

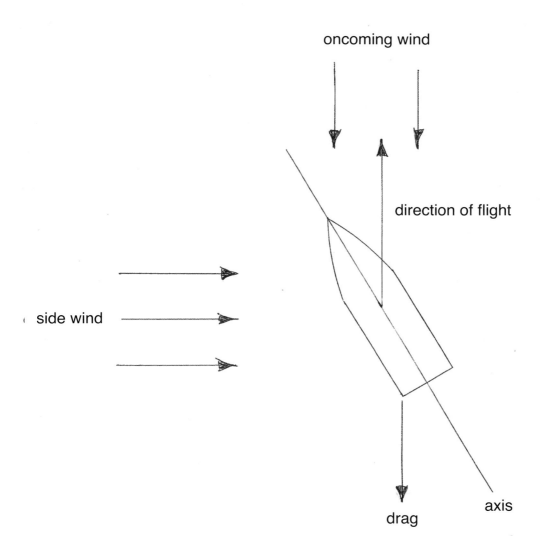

With a side-wind the head of the bullet tries to turn into the wind, but the drag causes it to go in the same direction as the wind.

Calculations like this can only ever be a guide, as what always becomes clear is that in reality wind is almost always unpredictable and its real effect is one of the great uncertainties of accurate shooting, especially at long range. All we can really do is try and bias the results in our favour by using the best form of bullet for the job in hand, and learning from experience to judge the wind the best we can.

BALLISTIC DRIFT

Ballistic drift, sometimes called spin-drift or gyroscopic drift, is caused by the gyroscopic effect of the bullet spinning on its axis. Actually it is a little more complicated than just the matter of bullet rotation, but for our purposes what is important is the following:

* For any particular bullet and speed of rotation the ballistic drift is a constant
* It only occurs in the horizontal plane
* A bullet with right-hand rotation will drift to the right, and a bullet with left-hand rotation will drift to the left

As an example, the ballistic drift of the venerable .303 British is 10in (25cm) at 1,000 yards; while the American 30-06 is 6.7in (17cm) with military bullets. However, because this drift is constant and we normally have the advantage of adjustable sights, it is in reality of little practical concern because we can make allowance for it as long as we are aware of its existence.

THE CORIOLIS EFFECT

The Coriolis effect is caused by the rotation of the earth and is what causes water going down a plughole to rotate in different directions either side of the equator. In practice, even at long range, it can be ignored because any inaccuracy caused by this is quite insignificant. Yet the theory is fascinating and has given rise to a charming, if untrue, story.

In theory the Coriolis effect occurs independently in both the vertical and horizontal plane. North of the equator any horizontal error is to the right, and vice versa south of the equator, and the effect becomes greater as one moves away from the equator towards the poles. Vertical error is zero firing north/south, but firing west means the bullet strikes low, and high if falling east. With an intercontinental ballistic missile this is probably important, but for the rifleman it has no great significance, although that is not what everyone always believed.

This is where we come to the story I mentioned a little earlier. It has been written that the British Army, in the days of an Empire that stretched across the globe, used rifles with a direction of twist appropriate to whichever hemisphere they were operating in. In other words, the rifles would have a left-hand twist in the northern hemisphere so the ballistic drift to the left would offset the Coriolis effect to the right, and the opposite twist rifling for use south of the equator. This is an interesting thought, but not true for a number of reasons, quite apart from the fact that the British Army tended towards high rates of fire, rather than ultra-long range accurate shooting. Logistically it would have been a nightmare and really impossible to manage, plus the ballistic drift is about five times greater than the Coriolis effect, even in the worst scenario.

There is a little known matter that may have prompted this story. The Lee Enfield rifle in its various marks, which served the British Army for generations, has left-hand twist rifling, but it may just be possible to find an ultra rare one with right-hand rifling. One of the UK's biggest arms manufacturers who produced complete Lee Enfield rifles apparently had one of their rifling machines with right-hand twist. It was suggested to me by a retired senior employee that when production was pressing, as in war time, and it was a case of 'needs must', it was 'quite likely' that small numbers of barrels were produced with right-hand twist which could have given some credibility to our little story. Sometimes things are not quite what they seem!

BULLET STABILITY IN FLIGHT

If a bullet did not spin about its axis the air pressure on its head would tip it over backwards,

CENTRE OF PRESSURE

CENTRE OF GRAVITY

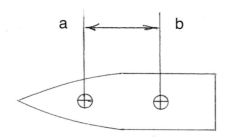

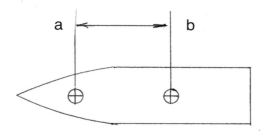

With a long bullet the centre of pressure
(a) and the centre of gravity (b) are further
apart than with a short bullet. This makes
the longer bullet more difficult to stabilize.

*A shorter bullet can be more rigid on its axis as the centre of pressure and centre
of gravity are not so far apart as with a longer bullet.*

then the same would occur against the base (now in front), making it tumble lengthways in flight around its centre of gravity. With a blunt-nosed bullet the centre of air pressure is a little further forward than with a pointed bullet, slightly exaggerating the tendency to tumble and, even with spin, making it just a little harder to stabilize.

The gyroscopic stability obtained by spinning the bullet gives it an axial rigidity that resists the tendency to tumble. This then leads us to the conclusion that a shorter bullet may be more rigid on its axis because the centre of pressure and centre of gravity are closer, with less 'leverage effect' trying to tip the bullet. This appears to be true. A longer bullet has more of a tendency to tip over, which is another reason why the spin rate has to be higher than with a short, stubby bullet.

Yet we are also aware by now that the longer bullet, if of a similar shape, is going to have a better ballistic coefficient and be more aerodynamically efficient. So, as with all these matters, to get the desired results for any particular form of shooting it becomes something of a ballistic balancing act.

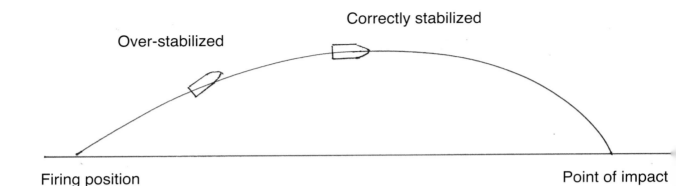

Over-stabilized

Correctly stabilized

Firing position

Point of impact

An over-stabilized bullet will fly head up. In the worst instance it may tumble at extreme range. Too much spin will exaggerate any errors in manufacture.

Over-spinning or over-stabilizing a bullet can be detrimental to accuracy, resulting in a nose-high attitude in flight that causes drag and the possibility of exaggerating any out of balance errors in manufacture.

If necessary, one way of increasing the spin for any barrel twist rate is to increase the velocity, although this has limitations, of course. Also it only works to a certain extent because as velocity increases so does the air resistance, and therefore the forces applied to the head of the bullet. Fortunately these forces usually have a lesser effect than the benefit from the increased spin rate. Then there is the matter of down-range performance, as the forward velocity of a bullet is reduced, due to air pressure, more quickly than its spin rate is diminished. So as the forces trying to tip the bullet around its centre of gravity are reducing, the spin rate imparting gyroscopic stability is, by comparison, increasing.

Just to complicate matters, there can be a slight drawback with 'over-spinning' the bullet. A bullet should always move nose-forwards along its flight path (or almost nose-forwards, as there is always a tendency to be slightly above the line of the trajectory); however, by spinning a bullet too fast it can have a very nose-high attitude, which then, rather like the matter of turning into a cross-wind, produces drag that diminishes performance.

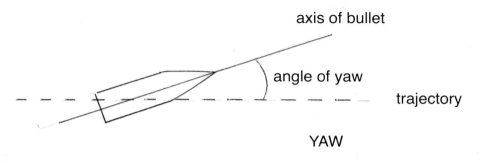

YAW

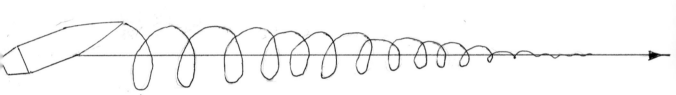

The gyroscopic effect of bullet rotation reduces the epicyclic motion as distance increases. (In layman's terms, the bullet 'wobbles' in flight.)

Yaw is the deviation of a bullet in its longitudinal axis from a straight line.

To the firearms student, yaw is the deviation of a bullet in its longitudinal axis from a straight line. When a bullet leaves the rifle muzzle its axis is not necessarily lined up along the trajectory, and the difference is the angle of yaw; also, in layman's terms, it wobbles in flight. If we could see what was happening, the nose of the bullet would appear to be rotating around the centre-line of its axis in an epicyclic motion resulting in a sort of corkscrew flight, although it still follows a stable flight path. This reduces as distance from the muzzle increases, and the gyroscopic effect of spin dampens out this motion. When it

flies true on its axis this is commonly known as 'going to sleep', which may be as little as thirty yards away or over 100, depending upon the cartridge, bullet, twist rate of rifling, and any adverse matters such as uneven muzzle erosion exaggerating the initial tendency for yaw.

If, in the early stages of flight when yaw is still quite high and a bullet meets resistance, say in the form of an animal, it can sometimes try to turn in its direction of rotation because the nose of the bullet is off-centre when it strikes. If it also strikes bone, especially a glancing blow, it may compound the problem, and can result in a wide

compression waves

A subsonic bullet pushes the compression
wave in front of it. The disturbed air moves
faster than the projectile.

The subsonic bullet pushes air compression waves in front of it.

but shallow 'off-centre' wound channel lacking in penetration. This effect is usually lessened when using soft-nosed bullets designed for rapid expansion. With a harder medium, shooting at ultra-short range, even with FMJ bullets, will result in less penetration than at longer distances when the tendency for yaw is reduced.

Weight distribution as a contributory factor in bullet stability is important, even back in the days of black powder and comparatively low velocities. A hollow nose or, in the case of one mark of .577 Snider bullet, a wooden plug in the nose, allowed the length-to-diameter ratio (aspect ratio, see page 69) to be increased a small amount without unduly increasing the weight, and contributed to improved accuracy. This method moved the centre of gravity back a very small amount, although still forward of the mid-point of the bullet. It is also an advantage with subsonic projectiles to have some drag at

the rear of the bullet, which is one contributory factor as to why long bore-riding bullets with the raised driving bands towards the base are usually accurate.

Take an extreme example of an ultra-low velocity projectile, the air-rifle pellet. It suffers in two ways: not only is it very low velocity but it is light in weight, or, to put it more scientifically, it has low mass. Stability is achieved by designs that are nose heavy, meaning that they have a forward centre of gravity, and a skirt at the rear that not only seals the bore but creates in-flight drag. Even if the spin imparted by the rifling is fairly low, this form of projectile has an in-built tendency to move through the air head forward.

Take a step back even further than this, and some readers may remember the darts available for smooth-bore airguns which had a flared tail like a brush. This acted like the tail of a shuttlecock, causing drag at the rear so that even with-out any gyroscopic stabilization the dart would still hit a target point first.

Once we move on to supersonic projectiles it becomes a different world, and the important matter of considerable influence in bullet stability is gyroscopic stabilization achieved by imparting spin. As we have previously seen, not all bullets give the same performance, and there is also this matter called 'aspect ratio' (the length-to-diameter ratio) of any projectile. A ball is 1:1, because its diameter is obviously the same as its length. Even a bullet that is short compared to its diameter may only give an aspect ratio of around 1.5:1, while a long streamlined bullet could be as much as 5:1. From this we can deduce that, for long-range shooting, a high aspect ratio is another desirable feature.

FLAT-BASE VERSUS BOAT-TAIL BULLETS

That important feature of the ultra-low velocity bullet, tail drag, is much less of a benefit with supersonic bullets. In fact any drag, such as caused by its basic form, has to be reduced as much as possible for long-range shooting as velocities increase. Why? Because air resistance increases as the square of velocity, so double the velocity and the air resistance increases fourfold. One part of the move towards reducing drag and to get a good ballistic coefficient is to have a very streamlined shape at the head of the bullet – but this is governed by the overall length. You cannot, for reasons of stability, have, say, a bullet that has a long tapered head with an ultra-short bear-

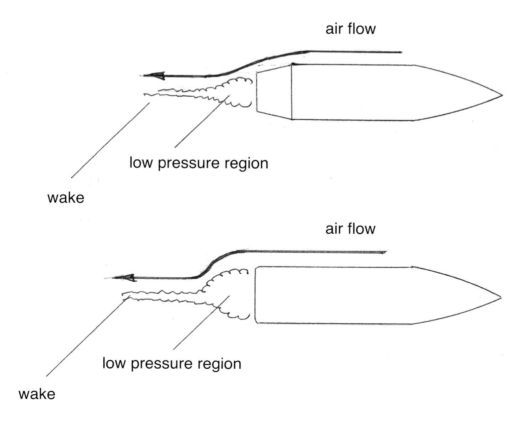

Air flow over boat-tail and flat-base bullets.

ing surface and therefore the centre of gravity nearly at the rear.

With that in mind, and having to work within practical constraints, reducing tail drag by forming a taper at the heel of the bullet (boat-tail) is a matter worthy of consideration. The small added benefit for the hand loader, especially when loading a reasonably large quantity of cartridges, is that it is easier to sit bullets into the neck of a cartridge case before seating if they are of boat-tail design.

What the boat tail does is increase the ballistic coefficient by reducing the base area of the bullet and therefore the low pressure area behind it. By comparison, a flat-base bullet has a low pressure area over the full cross-sectional area of the bullet, although the vacuum effect is less at the outside diameter than at the centre. With a boat-tail we score twice, because not only is the base area and drag reduced, but with a good design, the airflow follows the angled boat-tail.

I state 'with a good design' because there are limits, and the maximum practical angle for a boat-tail is 7 to 8 degrees. After that the airflow separates from the bullet and the drag is across the full area, as with a flat-base design. This, then, automatically places a restriction on the maximum length of a boat-tail, but this is anyway limited to no more than 0.8 calibres before it starts to have an adverse effect upon stability. A fairly new development is the rebated boat-tail bullet where there is a small step, typically 0.015in, before the taper. Whether this is of any real advantage seems yet to be proven.

Does this, then, mean that for all purposes the boat-tail bullet is superior? The answer is not always, and not for all purposes. When leaving the muzzle, the blast overtaking the bullet can have a more detrimental impact than with a flat base, because it can cause it to yaw more than a flat-base type and it will therefore take longer to fly true on its axis. As a boat-tail moves the centre of gravity and, for a given weight, slightly increases the length of the bullet, all other things being equal, it will theoretically (although not necessarily from a practical point of view) require a slightly faster rifling spin rate than a similar flat-base bullet.

Increase the spin rate and we get into the territory of exaggerating possible errors in manu-facture, such as any out-of-balance factor. You can add to this the fact that the boat-tail has more effect at velocities below 3,000ft/sec (915m/sec), because above this speed the air resistance at the nose is responsible for most of the drag – and then everything in the boat-tail garden seems not quite so rosy.

However, while of no advantage at short range, at long range, especially as velocities drop towards 2,500ft/sec (760m/sec), the boat-tail has a greater effect, and the better ballistic coefficient then starts to make itself felt. The result at longer ranges, say past 500 to 600 yards (460 to 550m), has the potential for better accuracy. The advantage therefore lies with the flat-base bullet at short ranges and the boat-tail for long-range shooting. For the stalker or hunter at comparatively short ranges, where target placement is always a little less precise and terminal performance of greater importance, the difference is not noticeable.

KNOCKOUT VALUE

No book on ballistics would be complete without some reference to 'knockout value', a subject that still generates lively debate and controversy. John Howard Taylor (Pondoro Taylor) was an elephant hunter during the interwar period, and wrote about his experiences in a practical and engaging manner. A man of enquiring mind, he included his ideas on practical striking energy, better known as knockout value (KOV), which was a comparison (rather than an actual value, as calculated muzzle energy) of the effectiveness of various cartridges.

Taylor's contention was that muzzle energy alone did not give a true indication of real performance, and that momentum and bullet diameter were also an important part of terminal performance. It should be remembered here that much of what he was using was of fairly large calibre and comparatively low velocity. Since those days others have refined Taylor's ideas and substituted either sectional density for bullet diameter or cross-sectional area. While the figures recorded differ, the general comparison between cartridges tends to follow the

Comparative Figures for KOV

Cartridge	bullet weight (grains)	velocity (ft/sec)	muzzle energy (ft/lb)	knockout value (KOV)
22-250 Remington	55	3,600	1,583.16	4.47
7mm Remington magnum	140	3,100	2,988.18	15.37
.308 Winchester	150	2,900	2,801.84	14.04
45-70 Government (black powder)	505	1,200	1,621.54	30.01

same trend. What it comes down to is that a big, heavy, slow bullet, which might on paper be a little deficient in muzzle energy compared to a lighter bullet of smaller calibre driven much faster, can perform just as well, and sometimes, for some purposes, even better.

It is true that rifle enthusiasts can be very fond of quoting muzzle energy as the sole indicator of terminal performance, although down-range energy would realistically be a better bet, and any figure quoted can only be the mean of those tested, as a calculated figure can never be exact, simply because there will be slight differences in velocity between each rifle and each cartridge. We have already touched upon the matter of sectional density being important relative to penetration (also bullet construction), so to a certain extent KOV appears to address some of the shortcomings of expressing performance just in terms of muzzle energy.

Momentum is the product of mass × velocity, so if we use the formula KOV = momentum × sectional density, we can produce some interesting figures for comparison, as the example in the table above shows.

On paper, the muzzle energy of this 22-250 Remington load is only 38.38ft/lb (52 joules) less than the black powder 45-70, a difference of a mere 2.37 per cent: thus for all practical applications it could be deemed to be the same, or as near as makes no difference. Yet the KOV of the 45-70 is 6.7 times greater than the 22-250 – and realistically, what you have to ask is, which would you use to shoot that bison?

The 7mm Remington magnum, even with its lighter, smaller calibre bullet, delivers both more muzzle energy and a higher KOV than the .308 Winchester because it has a better sectional density and a higher muzzle velocity. Examining the figures the muzzle energy is 6.23 per cent higher than the .308 Winchester, and the KOV is improved by 8.65 per cent.

This then brings us to the question, is knockout value a real factor to consider? Opponents of this idea will claim that a bullet passes through a body so quickly and is of such small mass that momentum can be discounted. They will go on to point out that the ballooning shock wave produced by a bullet's passage through a body is massive in comparison to any other feature. This is true with bullets travelling above 2,000ft/sec (615m/sec), which produce that so-called 'explosive effect', but what about lower velocities?

As a fan of the .450 calibre rifle, and having shot most species of deer from muntjac to red and wild boar with both smokeless powder and occasionally black powder loads, I can confirm that bigger, slow bullets of comparatively large diameter certainly do the job, but differently. The shock effect is diminished to the extent that the wound channel is usually no more than a ragged hole with an absence of burst blood vessels around it, or soft organs turned into little more than bloodied mush. To use a well known phrase in a slightly different manner, it gives a 'clean kill'.

Yet with a body shot, a .450 , especially if the bullet contacts bone, will sometimes slam a deer

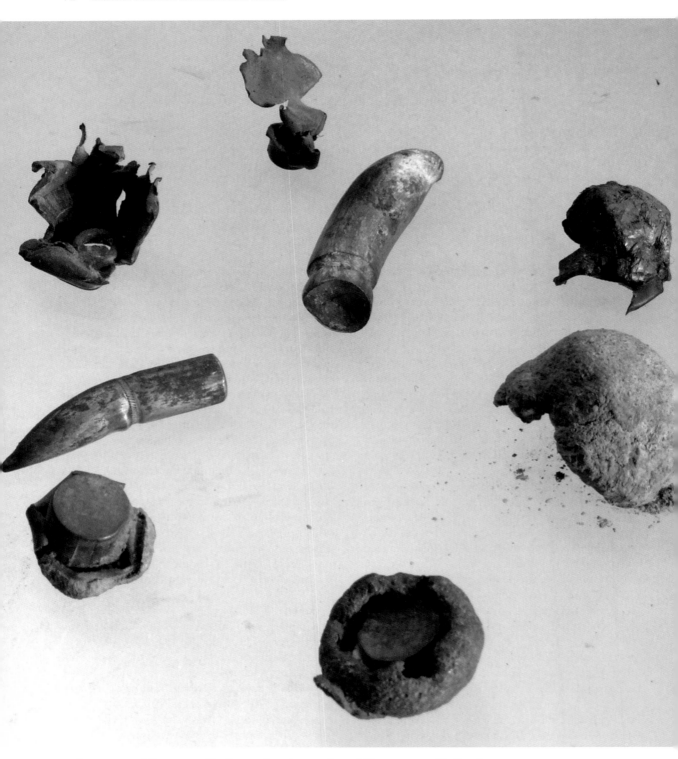

Bullets recovered from a sand bullet catcher showing how different types of bullet driven at varying velocities have different terminal characteristics.

to the ground with a similar visual effect to a lighter, smaller calibre bullet at much higher velocity which imparts that 'shock effect'.

Then it is worth considering that muzzle energy is itself only an indicator of performance, since energy on its own does not kill: it provides what we might call the 'drive' to the bullet. The properties of the bullet in terms of expansion, weight retention, penetration and fragmentation (or otherwise) all affect how the energy is transferred. Now we can begin to see why that 45-70 is always going to be a better bet on a big beast than the smaller calibre cartridge. The 55-grain bullet with its 'paper energy', similar to the 45-70, will lack penetration with a body shot on a large animal and may start to fragment early, thereby losing weight (reducing its mass), further adding to the lack of penetration. While the wound, due to the shock effect, will contain a lot of burst blood vessels and, as a result, bloodied meat, it might be rather shallow and not be fatal, or at least not immediately fatal.

On the other hand the 505-grain 45-70 bullet of theoretically similar muzzle energy has several advantages: it has a much better sectional density, giving good, and if not good, at least reasonable penetration, it is usually blunt-nosed, which has a better initial striking effect, and due to the comparatively low velocity, it will be less subject to any form of fragmentation, thereby retaining much of its original mass.

Based on my experiences, my conclusion is that with bullets driven at lower velocities, say between 1,250ft/sec (380m/sec) and 1,950ft/sec (595m/sec), and of over .35in calibre and more than 200 grains in weight, the KOV formula is a useful comparative guide. In practice I have found that velocities around 1,950ft/sec and bullets of 350 grains for .450 calibre give the best all-round practical performance, while for smaller animals, a 300-grain bullet with a large hollow point and even of poor sectional density works very well, and still keeps meat damage within acceptable limits compared to, say, a .243 Winchester even using comparatively heavy-for-calibre 100-grain bullets.

The down side is a higher trajectory and, with some of the 'hotter' loads, a fairly substantial recoil. Still, it is all interesting stuff and worth the look on other stalkers' faces when they ask 'What are you going to do with that cannon — blow them to pieces?' The reality, of course, is just the opposite, but even faced with the evidence it is difficult for some shooters to comprehend just why this should be.

Chapter 4
Practical Matters Affecting Performance and Accuracy

Much of this chapter concerns matters of interest to those enthusiasts who make their own bullets, usually of cast lead, and sometimes swaged or jacketed. Just because a bullet may be intended for comparatively low velocity use, say at a muzzle velocity below 2,000ft (609m)/sec, this does not mean one can neglect the attention to detail necessary for good quality production, which in turn reflects upon performance. To show how things can go wrong, a series of experiments has been recorded which, while they somewhat exaggerate the respective faults, do show the real effect upon accuracy.

THE REQUIREMENTS OF AN ACCURATE BULLET

It is obvious that the requirements of accuracy of manufacture do not concern just single bullets: each one in a whole batch has to be virtually identical. Then, allowing for human error, accurate loading, a good rifle and any external influences, they should strike the target in almost the same place. A properly made and potentially accurate bullet is one that is concentric to its axis, with its base square to the axis, of even density so there is no gyroscopic out of balance, and of the same form, hardness and weight as all the others in the batch.

Most home-made bullets will be produced from lead or a lead-based alloy cast in a two-piece mould, and moulds do vary in quality. Usually noticeable is a fine flashing line where the molten lead tries to enter the joint between the two mating faces of the mould blocks. All moulds will leave a thin 'witness' line, which is acceptable, but an obviously raised narrow ridge of lead, albeit quite rare, may mean a mould to

be avoided (see note below). Also, while outside the scope of this book, it is nonetheless important to note that a constant furnace temperature is a requirement, as is the composition, if a lead alloy is used.

To get the very best results, the composition of any alloy, usually tin/lead, should be known, as this will affect hardness, weight and, to a small extent, overall dimensions. The latter is a dimensional change usually of such insignificance that it can be ignored, and comes about because various lead alloys will exhibit different contraction rates upon cooling. However, it is something worth noting for those occasions when the desired results are not achieved, but everything else with the bullets seems fine.

Note: Flashing occurs only along the mould joint line and is especially obvious if the lead and mould are too hot. Sprue occurs where the lead is poured into the mould, and this is normally cut off by the action of opening the mould gate.

Bullet Sizing

Cast bullets can be slightly oval, usually along the mould joint line, which means they do not meet the requirements for proper concentricity. How much this might impact on actual accuracy of performance is difficult to evaluate, because upon firing they will 'bump up' and form to the bore – but a bullet touching at two points in the lead is technically a bad idea. Realistically it is likely that with either a pure lead or soft (a relative term) lead alloy bullet, the effect will be of small significance. It is equally likely that, with much harder lead alloys, it may be detrimental to performance so it is always best to use a 'sizer' die to eliminate any

Cast and unsized bullet loaded for 40-90 Sharps showing just one of two contact points in the lead of the chamber.

possibility of a fault in this area, while at the same time ensuring the correct bullet diameter.

The one type of bullet where sizing does not do a complete job is the bore-riding design, where around half of the length of the bullet is calibre size and the rest is raised driving bands. Typically for a .450 calibre rifle this would mean the bore-riding section would be 0.449/0.450in, with the raised driving bands 0.457/0.458in. When pushed through a sizer die, only the driv-

ing band makes contact, but with this design it is something one has to live with.

Checking Concentricity

For checking concentricity, a dial indicator mounted on its own right-angled precision base, or with a magnetic base on a surface table, will suffice. Most industrial dial indicators measure down to 0.001in (one thousandth of an inch), some to 0.0005in (half a thousandth of an inch), and the latter, if one can be found, is preferable.

The simplest way of checking is to mark the bullet in four equally spaced places, then roll it under the dial indicator in the first position to be checked, and set it at zero. When rolling it under in the other three positions, if the dial indicator reads other than zero, this shows some eccentricity or ovality of the bullet. This is not confined to cast bullets, and it can be an interesting exercise to check jacketed ones just to compare makes.

Another method which is a bit fiddly but is possible with really large calibre bullets is to rotate the bullet in a V block mounted directly under the dial indicator. With large bullets it is not a problem, but small bullets and short fingers can make it an impossible task to get anything like consistent results.

The other aspect of concentricity does not directly concern the bullet, but how it is held in the cartridge case.

Base Squareness

Cast bullet base squareness to the axis of the bore is entirely a matter that comes down to the mould quality of manufacture, always assuming the casting process has been carried out correctly. It is very rarely a problem, and a check of a few bullets will confirm their accuracy or otherwise. The very best way to check this is by using a shadowgraph, which usually means cadging some time on an industrial unit; nowadays these are very compact. Sitting on its base and rotated in increments through 360 degrees, and moved up against the graticule on the shadow-

Checking a bullet for form and concentricity under a dial indicator.

Checking an 8-bore Paradox bullet for concentricity or roundness by rotating it in a Vee block under a dial indicator.

graph, will show any 'lean', indicating the base is out of square. It also shows up the whole form of the bullet magnified, so all sorts of interesting dimensional checks can be taken.

Failing access to a shadowgraph, we can adopt the gunsmith's traditional method used to check if shotgun barrels are 'on the face' (breech ends of barrels to standing breech) – in other words, looking for light through a gap. While seemingly simple, if not crude, it is possible using this method to detect a gap of a few thousandths of an inch. The light source needs to be a constant 'soft' light, and under the right conditions natural daylight will suffice.

With the bullet set up on an accurate surface, such as a surface plate, using a set square against the vertical side of the bullet, any 'lean' or 'bend'

(bent bullets are not unknown) can be detected. If a sliver of light becomes apparent between the blade of the set square and the side of the bearing surface of the bullet, and especially if it alters as the bullet is moved around, there is some inaccuracy in manufacture. With any of these checks it is necessary to ensure that a flat-base bullet is not sitting on any sprue left from the hole where the lead is poured into the mould.

Once again we come to the question of how much does this matter, what degree of inaccuracy is acceptable, and when does it become unacceptable? The answer has to be that we do not always know; but what we do know is that the nearer a bullet is to being of perfect manufacture ('perfect' being a theoretical, rather than a practical goal), the better is its performance.

Checking a 4-bore bullet for base squareness against a set square.

After that it comes down to performance on the target, and what one often finds is that a shorter, stubby bullet with some errors in manufacture is less affected than an imperfect long, slim bullet.

Experiment

This experiment investigated what effect an out-of-square bullet base has on accuracy.

Equipment: Pedersoli reproduction 1874 Sharps rifle fitted with a riflescope and shooting from a rest. Range 100 metres (108 yd), load 55 grains, Swiss number three black powder, priming charge 5 grains of Hercules Reloder 7 separated from main charge by air-mail paper wad impregnated with saltpetre. Bullet 515 grain (Lyman mould) alloy lead 90 per cent, tin 10 per cent by weight. Angle to base 10 degrees, weight 480 grains, weight reduction 6.8 per cent.

Results:
Average muzzle velocity 1,162ft/sec (354m/sec)
Extreme spread 22ft/sec (6.7m/sec)
Bullet muzzle rotational speed (1:18 twist)
774.7rps (revolutions per second)
Distance 100 metres (108yd)

With the angled base in the twelve o'clock position when loaded, the bullet struck high (just off the target, in fact). At three o'clock they went right, at nine o'clock to the left at an average distance error of 19¼in (49cm), while angular error was sometimes erratic.

Re-testing at 50m (54yd) to keep all the bullet strikes on target and loading with the angled base at six o'clock, the bullets struck low and to the left, 7½in (19cm) from the true zero, with bullets having the base square to the axis.

Bullets manufactured with base square to axis and angled base.

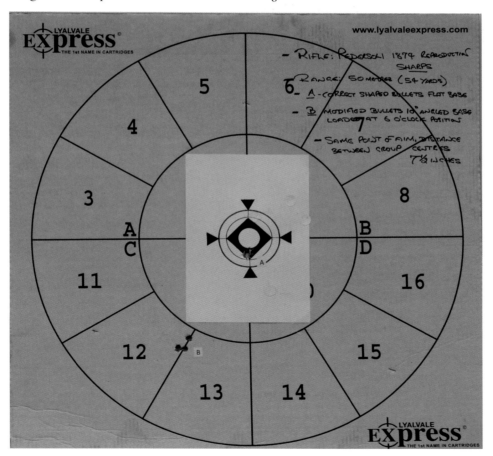

Shot at 50m (54yd), when loaded in the same position (within practical limitations) the bullet strikes produced a better group than expected, even though the point of impact had shifted 7½in (19cm) from the true zero.

The Pedersoli reproduction 1874 Sharps fitted with a quarter rib and riflescope that performed well in the angled base tests.

Conclusion: As shown, bullets loaded with the angled base in the same plane strike the target in a similar position, but may produce a larger group due to any angular error when loading. In reality loading would be quite random, as would the results.

Taking as an example a bullet with the angled base in the three o'clock position, when loaded, meant it appeared to move in that direction. However, with a 28in barrel (less nominally 2in chamber) this means, when exiting the muzzle at 1½ turns from the breech, the angled base was in the opposite position to when it was loaded. Therefore it would appear that it is the muzzle gases tending to push past the bullet along the angled face that tips the bullet in its final direction and exaggerates the yaw.

The errors generated by an out-of-square bullet base were much more dramatic than expected, therefore one can conclude that a well finished base, square to the axis of the bullet, is vitally important.

Bullet Weight

Consistency of weight in any batch of bullets is very important. It does not matter if the weight of a bullet adds up to an odd number of grains as long as the others are nearly identical. An acceptable tolerance is a matter of judgment based on practical experiment and experience. What one has to remember is that a figure of, say, five grains difference with a 150-grain bullet represents 3.333 per cent of its weight, but the same five grains with a 500-grain bullet is only 1 per cent of its weight. Based on my experiences, if weight differences are kept within +/ −1 grain, that is a good practical starting figure to use as a guide.

Weighing most bullets is not a problem as powder scales can be used. If the bullet weight exceeds the capacity of the scale a piece of lead can be attached to the arm of the scale furthest from the pivot to increase the range. While this is not a method of obtaining a true weight, as we are interested in comparative weights between bullets it is quite acceptable.

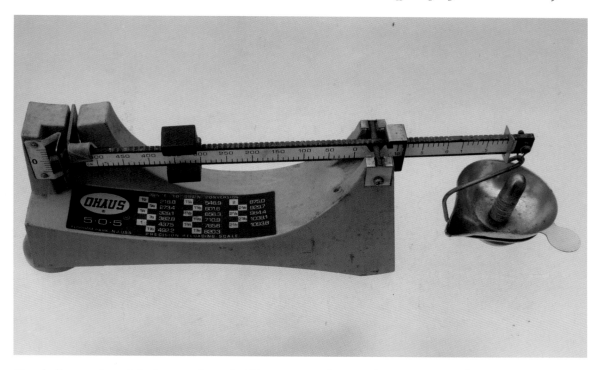

Most bullets can be weighed on powder scales. Where it is simply a weight comparison and bullets exceed the range of the scale a weight can be added to the arm.

Bullet out of Balance

A bullet rotating in flight at high speed needs to be of even density and material construction (which also affects weight), otherwise it will be unbalanced and the centrifugal forces involved may produce what might be described as a wobble in its flight. This arises because the axis of the bullet is no longer the same as that which it needs to rotate around to be in balance, while the rotation of the bullet produced by the rifling on the bearing surface is true to the bullet's actual axis regardless of any out-of-balance factor.

What we have is a shift in the centre of balance, and we look at it as a conflict of interests where the heavier part of the bullet is trying to throw itself off line to one side. If we could see this in flight it would look (actually for opposite reasons) rather like a spinning top when it slows down and the diminishing gyroscope effect is struggling to keep it vertical. With the bullet it is the speed of rotation that is exaggerating the fault, as any model maker rotating an out-of-balance crankshaft in a lathe can testify when at cer-

tain speeds it seems capable of almost vibrating the machine off its stand.

While there is no ready method of checking the gyroscopic balance of a bullet, differing weights can be an indicator of a potential problem, and if a bullet rolled across a flat level surface always stopped in the same place this would be heavy side down (or due to distortion). The error involved is usually too small to detect by such primitive methods, but we can see the effect on accuracy by practical experiments.

Experiment

To see how bullets out of balance compare to those in balance

Equipment: To obtain out-of-balance bullets exhibiting the same fault, swaged bullets of even material density were drilled through the base and the holes filled with fibreglass resin, which is lighter than the lead removed but retains the structural integrity of the bullet. The unmodified .450 calibre bullet, less the paper patching,

Bullets modified out of balance. From left: the basic .450in swaged bullet; a hole drilled out and filled with resin; a modified bullet paper-patched to 0.457in.

weighed 412 grains, and the modified bullet 385 grains, making a weight difference of 6.55 per cent; powder load was 45g Reloder 7, ⅛in fibre wad under bullet, distance tested 100m.

Results:
Average muzzle velocity 1,743ft/sec (531m/sec)
Extreme spread 57ft/sec (17m/sec)
Bullet muzzle rotational speed (at muzzle, 1:20 twist) 1,045rps (revolutions per second)
Distance 100 metres (108yd)

With the bullets and cartridge cases marked to identify the modified area, all were loaded with the light side of the bullet in the three o'clock position (heavy side nine o'clock). Strikes on the target were at eleven o'clock and 11¾in (30cm)

from the group of unmodified bullets. With a 1:20 twist and 22in) barrel, less the chamber (nominal 2in), means the bullets were exiting the muzzle in virtually the same out-of-balance position as when they were loaded.

Conclusion:

* Being loaded with the out-of-balance error in the same position gave better grouping than expected. However, loading each one in exactly the same way, even with marked up cartridges cases, is not really possible, and there is always going to be a small angular error. We can assume, therefore, that had the angular location of the drilled hole been exactly aligned each time, the grouping would have been tighter.

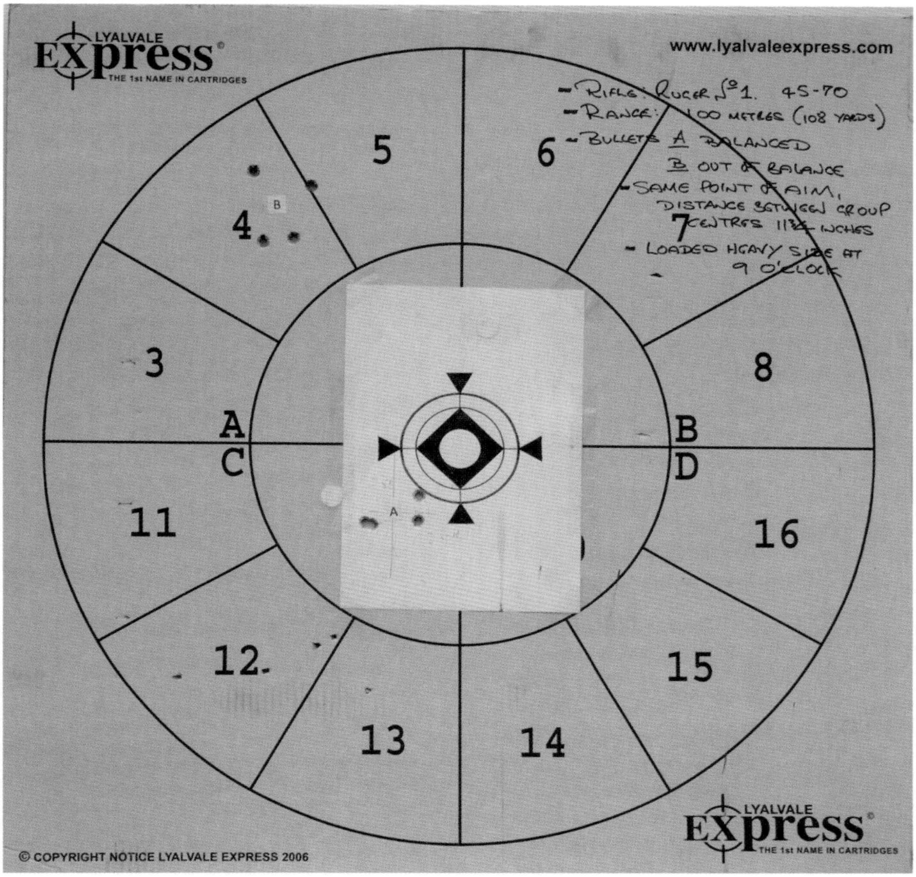
LYALVALE
Express
THE 1st NAME IN CARTRIDGES
www.lyalvaleexpress.com
-RIFLE: RUGER Nº1. 45-70
-RANGE: 100 METRES (108 YARDS)
-BULLETS A BALANCED
B OUT OF BALANCE
-SAME POINT OF AIM,
DISTANCE BETWEEN GROUP
CENTRES 11¾ INCHES
- LOADED HEAVY SIDE AT
9 O'CLOCK
3
4
5
6
7
8
11
12
13
14
15
16
A
B
C
D
© COPYRIGHT NOTICE LYALVALE EXPRESS 2006

The results of shooting out-of-balance bullets. These were the best groups achieved. Measurement between groups was 11¾in (29.8cm) at the same point of aim.

* At the distances tested it would not be surprising to find these slightly lighter bullets striking high, but the real effect is greatly exaggerated by the bullet having one side heavier than the other.
* Why did they not strike to the left, but in line with the original group, even if just slightly high? The barrel had a right-hand twist, the effect of which would be to 'throw' the heavy side not just left, but high, due to its direction of rotation. Reversing the loading technique (heavy side at three o'clock) pushed the groups low and to the right. In other words, reversing the error when loading will produce the opposite effect.

Bullet Hardness

The hardness of a lead or lead alloy bullet in part determines the maximum velocity it can be propelled up the barrel without depositing lead in the bore, which has a detrimental effect upon accuracy. In the worst instance stripping across the rifling can occur so the bullet tumbles because no spin has been imparted. But it is not always quite that simple, since accelerating a bullet quickly at the start of its ballistic journey may cause stripping, where a slower (in relative terms) start with a more gradual build-up of velocity could conceivably mean a better muzzle velocity and no problems. That does not alter the basic fact, though, that a cast or swaged bullet intended for higher velocities needs to be

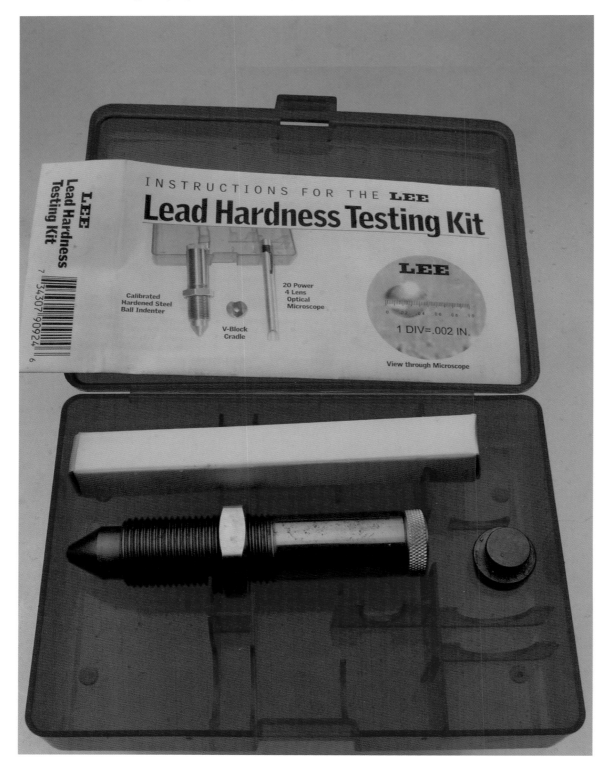

A Poldi-type hardness tester for checking cast bullet hardness.

harder to hold the rifling to avoid problems, or paper patched, a process which would normally be used with softer bullets.

Just how hard an unpatched bullet needs to be very much depends upon whether the propellant is black powder, a duplex load or smokeless powder. The diameter and, to a much lesser extent, the length of the bullet and therefore twist rate of the rifling all have an influence on what happens.

This very much becomes a matter for individual testing, but the important issue is to know the bullet's hardness as a basis to work from, and that each batch is substantially the same. This can be achieved with the aid of a Poldi-type hardness tester.

FURTHER MATTERS AFFECTING PERFORMANCE

Oil in the Chamber

As with any rifle barrel, the chamber should always be dry and clean prior to use. Oil in the chamber, or lubricant left on a cartridge case from the reloading press, will mean the case does not hold and seal against the chamber wall properly when fired – rather, it will tend to slam back against the breech face.

Too much oil in the chamber and we come upon another problem that can cause actual damage to the rifle. When fired, the oil will be forced along the cartridge case, and upon each subsequent firing, tends to accumulate in an area level where the base of the bullet sits in the cartridge case. Eventually this build-up of lubricant in the one area can form a ring bulge in the chamber, which in turn can make extraction of the fired case very difficult, if not impossible without using a cleaning rod from the muzzle end to knock out the cartridge case.

It is very doubtful whether such damage could occur when using black powder as a propellant, but it is quite possible for this to happen with the higher breech pressures achieved with smokeless powders.

The result of oil left in the chamber. The right-hand cartridge case shows indents from oil migrating towards where the base of the bullet sits in the case. The left-hand example is the next stage, where oil has ring-bulged the chamber.

Neck Sizing / Turned Necks

One option to aid more consistent performance which is open to the hand loader is sizing just the neck back to the original dimensions. This is best carried out on once-fired cases, meaning those fired in the rifle for which they are intended to be reused. This has several advantages, such as a considerable reduction in brass flow, a case that fits the chamber correctly, elimination of any headspace problems, and a bullet in better alignment with the axis of the bore.

The only thing that can then have an adverse affect is neck eccentricity, where material is thicker on one side of the neck than the other. Exactly how much a bullet being held a thousandth of an inch or so out of line will affect consistency of accuracy is difficult to determine, and it is likely the actual form of the bullet ogive and angle of the lead into the rifling may make matters slightly better or worse. However, in this pursuit of ballistic perfection it is something worthy of attention.

The answer, of course, is to turn the outside of the neck to produce a uniform thickness, but this must not be overdone otherwise the case will not seal properly in the neck area and in extreme circumstances the neck tension that holds the bullet in place may be reduced to such a degree that the bullet can move in the case with clumsy handling or especially in a magazine when subject to recoil.

The other, more subtle effect of reduced neck tension means reduced, or at least altered, performance due to changes in breech pressure, as the bullet may be released from the neck earlier than would happen with the correct hold of the neck on the bullet.

Sizing a neck for a specially dimensioned (tight) chamber. The neck rotates on the mandrel and the tool on the outside reduces the diameter and ensures even wall thickness.

One way out of this potential dilemma is to have a specially dimensioned chamber with what is simply called a tight neck: in other words, the neck area of the chamber is of slightly reduced diameter. This has the advantage that a case neck can be turned concentric to fit, leaving a calculated clearance. The disadvantage is that commercially dimensioned ammunition will not fit or, if it were possible to force it into the chamber, dangerously high pressures would result. Tight neck chambers have to be declared when submitted for proof and the dimensions will be marked on the barrel.

Note: Going back to simple neck sizing, this is especially useful with cartridges such as the rimmed .303 British, which has more clearance in the front of the shoulder and the neck area of the chamber than would be normal for a commercial design of cartridge. Allegedly to allow for possibly dirty ammunition to still chamber in the heat of battle, it is a nuisance to the hand loader who wishes to get the most life out of the cartridge cases.

When first fired the neck expands and the shoulder moves a little way forwards. Constant full length resizing back to standard dimensions can soon lead to failure of the case at the base of the neck. Neck sizing stopped just short of the expanded shoulder so the cartridge is a snug fit, but still headspaces on the rim will leave a slight raised ring in front of the shoulder; this looks a little odd, but greatly reduces any possibility of case cracking in this area, as well as producing better axial alignment of the bullet to the bore.

Cartridge Case Problems that Affect Performance

It is well known that cartridge cases intended for reloading should be sorted by make, otherwise ballistic performance may differ. Different makes and tolerances in manufacture, leading to changes in head and wall thickness, primer hole size and finish, all have an influence, especially those that affect the internal case capacity and, to a certain extent, overall strength or case rigidity.

The same problems, sometimes on a larger scale, can apply with distorted or malformed

Case head separation, usually due to excess headspace and resizing the cartridge case back to standard dimensions for further use.

The circular shiny marks on the head of this cartridge case are indications of zero or even tight headspace.

cases, usually as a result of reloading. Common faults are cases that are either too short or too long, and less obvious matters, for example a build-up of brass inside the case, such as where the shoulder joins the neck.

Rimless cartridges that are produced with the case slightly short from shoulder to head can display all the symptoms of excess headspace and the problems of case failure associated with that fault. The same sort of case formed slightly over-long can also display visible faults remarkably similar to excess headspace, including case head separation.

This happens in a bolt-action rifle, because even if the cartridge is slightly overlength it can still sometimes be chambered by the forceful camming action of the bolt. With the shoulder of the cartridge hard in the chamber, the force exerted by the bolt squeezes the head of the case forwards, and to accommodate this albeit tiny movement, the case bulges sideways at the point where the web of the case head joins the wall.

If this is repeated over a few firings, especially following full length resizing, the head will eventually start to separate. On cursory examination it will have the appearance of excess headspace, but the giveaway that it is the opposite fault (apart from the difficulty in loading) will be shiny annular marks on the case head in the region of the headstamp. This is caused by the bolt face being held hard against the case head and rotating against it as the bolt is closed. It is possible that this semi-rotary force is also a small contributory factor in the eventual case-head failure.

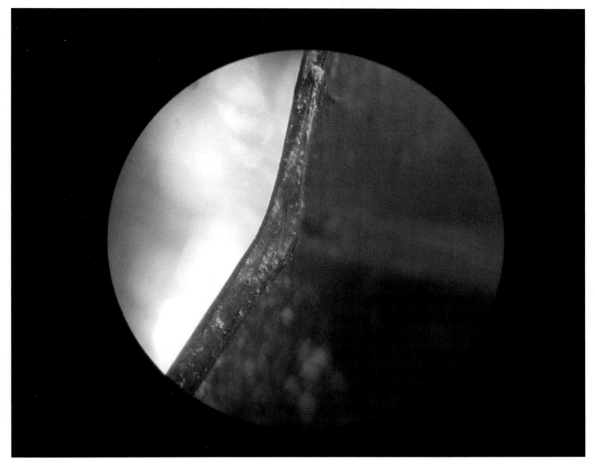

Cutaway cartridge case (×24) showing the thickening of the brass where the neck meets the shoulder.

The other matter concerning case length is where the neck 'grows' forwards due to brass flow. The effect varies with different cartridges, and the degree of neck lengthening can be difficult to predict. As a general guide, it is less obvious with cartridges operating at lower breech pressures, and one of the claims for steep-shouldered designs such as the Ackley Improved is a reduction in this problem. But the real culprit in this gradual neck lengthening is constant full length resizing.

It can be possible to chamber a rimless or rimmed cartridge where the neck is longer than the design tolerance, and this can have adverse effects on both pressure and velocity. The mouth of the case forced into the lead of the chamber can effectively crimp itself on to the bullet. This means that, unlike a normal crimp, not only is the bullet held more tightly, but there is no room for neck expansion to release the bullet on firing; as a result, high, even dangerously high, pressures can be generated, and if the neck lengths vary, so may pressure, velocity and accuracy.

The aspect of brass flow that is not immediately obvious is the build-up in thickness of the case wall where the shoulder joins the neck. It can also occur where the case wall joins the shoulder, although usually to a lesser extent, and it has little impact compared to the thickening at the base of the neck, which, in the worst instance, can be visible as a raised annular ring. Cartridge cases that have been subjected to considerable reforming and shortening from another type, resulting in an unusually thick-walled case at the shoulder, often seem particularly susceptible to this fault when it is likely to become a problem.

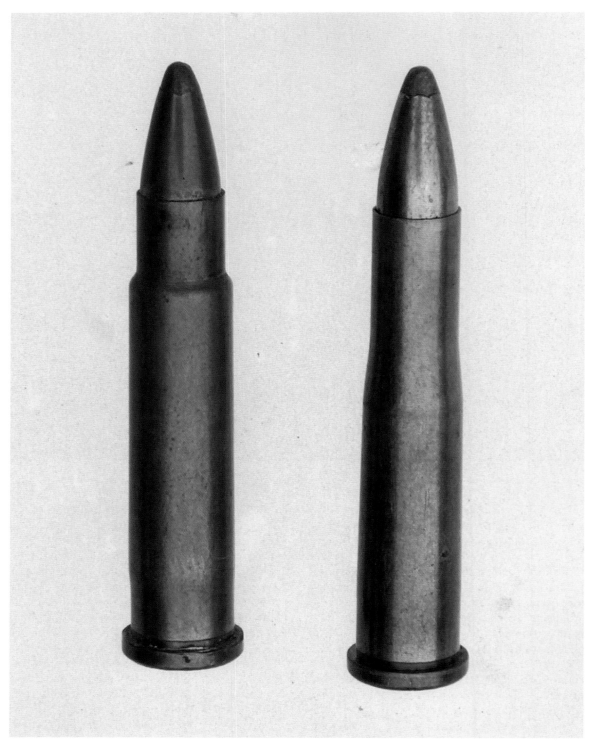

Reforming quite extensively the standard .22 Hornet cartridge case (left) to the K Hornet requires good brass that is not brittle.

If a bullet, usually one of flat-base design, is seated past this protruding ring, it can produce problems. This starts with external neck expansion at the base of the neck due to the restricted internal area. The cartridge may then headspace at this point rather than on the shoulder, even reducing the headspace to the point that it is tight to shut the breech, with the problems that can follow on from that.

If this happens it also means that the bullet is held more tightly than intended, with the additional problem of a lack of space for adequate neck expansion at the base of the neck, all contributing to extra high breech pressure. With a boat-tail bullet the problem may not occur and the case distortion may not become obvious, simply because the taper at the base of the bullet may provide sufficient clearance to miss the restriction.

Brittle Cartridge Cases

Brass cartridge cases that have been overworked by being resized many times can become brittle. This usually occurs in the neck area, and eventually tiny cracks will become visible. Even if not overworked, it will be found that some makes of cartridge case are less tolerant to being either reworked many times or reshaped, such as by fire-forming. Something like the .22 Hornet being reformed to a .22 K Hornet, where the shoulder is moved and considerably reshaped, requires fairly soft brass otherwise there can be a high rate of cases splitting.

To avoid this sort of problem the neck area of a cartridge case can be annealed – in the most basic terms, softened. However, this must not be overdone as a cartridge case that is annealed for too much of its length will expand upon firing but not contract to allow good extraction.

.303 British cartridge cases in a pan, necks marked with a heat-sensitive crayon. About ¾ inch (2cm) depth of water will be added.

A simple method used for years is to place clean, well polished cartridge cases in a shallow pan of water to prevent the spread of heat. For something the length of, say, a 30-06 case, about ⅝in depth of water is sufficient. The necks are then heated with a small gas torch until a bluish colour is seen to move towards the shoulder. Then there are two options: the first is to just leave them to cool, the other, and more favoured method, is to tip the cartridge cases over into the water to preserve the grain structure of the brass in its correctly annealed state.

A more sophisticated temperature control method is to use something like a Tempilstick, a well known brand name for a heat-sensitive crayon. Using the water-pan method but watching the crayon melt or change colour (being partly colour-blind I prefer the melting type) is more precise, and a Tempilstick that melts at 650°F gives good results.

When case-neck cracking does occur it is usually detected upon examination prior to reloading. If not, it may become obvious when seating the bullet as the neck can have insufficient tension to hold the bullet firmly, or the very act of seating the bullet in the neck will push a 'micro crack' open, making it quite visible.

If it evades the various check stages to finish up as a loaded cartridge in a rifle, is that at all dangerous? The answer has to be possibly, much depending upon the condition and dimensions of the rifle chamber and the type of action.

The accompanying photograph shows a 6.5 × 55 Swedish cartridge case where the neck failed in use. After firing the user felt that something was wrong and was more than a little concerned about the smoke exiting the breech area even before the bolt was opened. Upon examination the bullet was found to be stuck about a third of the way up the barrel. Visible from inside the neck of the cartridge case were two lines of cracks. Externally, as can be seen from the photograph, it now showed signs of gas erosion, and there were carbon deposits the full length of the cartridge case.

It would appear that the leakage occurred at a very early stage in the ignition/burn process, so service pressures were not reached and therefore the cartridge case did not form a complete seal, with a resultant loss of pressure.

A 6.5 × 55 Swedish cartridge case where the neck failed initially due to cracking. Later tests indicated that the lack of sealing was undoubtedly exaggerated by using a very light powder charge.

An occurrence like this is very rare, but the chances of the unusual happening are always with us. The moral of the story for hand loaders must be to make sure cartridge cases are in faultless condition as this is your breech seal, holding at bay several tons pressure of hot gases.

EXTERNAL FACTORS AFFECTING ACCURACY

Canted Sights

Sights, usually riflescopes with their fairly high mount, if not set up square to the axis of the barrel, are a recipe for inaccuracy. Most sporting rifle shooters fit the riflescope so that the reticule appears correct with the rifle mounted to the shoulder. However, right-handed shooters tend to can the rifle to the left – the opposite for left-handed shooters – so the vertical reticule is not then in line with the axis of the bore. With a rifle set up in this manner by a right-handed shooter, the line of flight of the bullet will drift to the left of the line of sight. The same effect occurs if the sights are mounted correctly but the rifle held canted.

Experiment

This experiment was to determine the detrimental effect of canting.

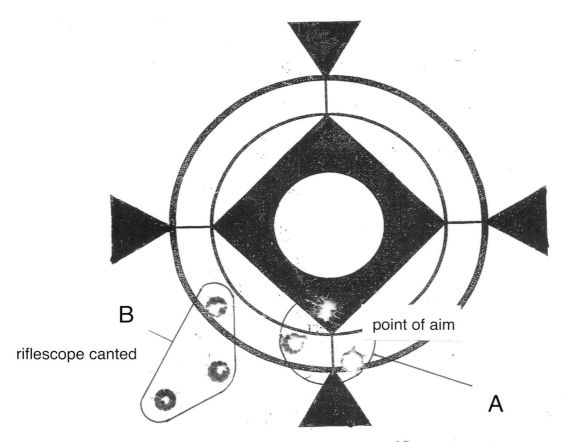

B

riflescope canted

point of aim

A

riflescope vertical to axis of bore

Canting the rifle but still using the same point of aim moved the bullet strikes 1¾in (4.45cm) to the left.

Equipment: Sako rifle chambered .308 Winchester fitted with riflescope and bipod. Test shots taken at 100 metres (108yd).
a) Rifle with reticule in the normal position and sitting level on bipod.
b) Rifle with support under one leg of bipod to provide canting.

Results: Even with the same point of aim, the group with the rifle canted is 1¾in (4.45cm) to the left of the group representing true zero.

Conclusion: Any canting, either of rifle and riflescope, or the riflescope canted relative to the rifle, is detrimental to best accuracy.

The Fitting of Bipods

The fitting of a bipod is generally thought to be an aid to accurate shooting, but it is not always the benefit it might seem. In fairly rare cases the weight of the rifle, plus most often a sound moderator, might combine to cause interference between the forend and barrel if clearance was already minimal, and this can have a detrimental effect upon accuracy as it will change the vibration pattern of the barrel.

The other, more common cause of inaccuracy – or accurate groups but moving to a different zero point – is zeroing off a bipod compared to some other means of support. With something like the low-powered .22 rimfire cartridge there may be no discernible difference between zeroing off a bipod or supported with a sandbag. However, even something comparatively modest such as the .243 Winchester cartridge can show variations in the point of bullet impact between these two methods of supporting a rifle.

Then when using a bipod there is always the matter of the nature of the support under its feet. That old favourite of the vermin shooter, the Land Rover bonnet, is not the sturdiest platform and this can affect accuracy. Also it can be compounded by the method currently popular of holding just the pistol grip of the rifle stock with the trigger finger hand, while supporting the toe of the stock (for elevation purposes) with the other hand. This leaves the rifle without any downward steadying load (apart from its own weight), particularly on the forend.

Practical rifle shooters who are aware of this will sometimes use the sling to apply a downward load, even when shooting off a bipod.

A further complication is whether or not a sound moderator is fitted. The additional weight of the sound moderator, the distribution or location of that weight, and its efficiency when acting as a muzzle brake, can affect accuracy. The difference can be small and will vary with different rifles and sound moderators, but when shooting off a bipod without any additional downward load or firm hold at the forend, the use of a sound moderator may prove beneficial.

Experiment

This experiment was to compare the effect of zeroing with the following:

a) Rifle fitted with a bipod and sound moderator shooting off a wooden bench, with the rifle held only at the pistol grip.
b) As a), but without the sound moderator.
c) Rifle with a sound moderator, supported on 'rabbit ear' sandbags, on a wooden bench, with the shooter holding both the pistol grip and the forend.

Equipment: Sako rifle chambered .308 Winchester, 21inch medium heavy sporter barrel. TLD over-barrel type sound moderator with experimental seven baffles, weight 24.4oz (690g), Harris bipod. Ammunition: Norma cartridge cases, CCI 200 primers, bullet Speer 168 gn Gold Match, powder charge 42 gns Vhitavouri N140, average velocity 2,550ft/sec (777m/sec).

Results: (All same the point of aim)
a) Three shot group on the centre line of the target, maximum group error centre to centre ⅜in (1cm).

b) Three shot group, centre of group ⅜in (1cm) to the left of group (a) and 1in (2.5cm) lower. Centre to centre group error 1½in (3.8cm).

OPPOSITE AND OVERLEAF: *These targets indicate the advisability of zeroing a rifle in the manner it is likely to be used, and the desirability of a suitably sturdy base to support a bipod.*

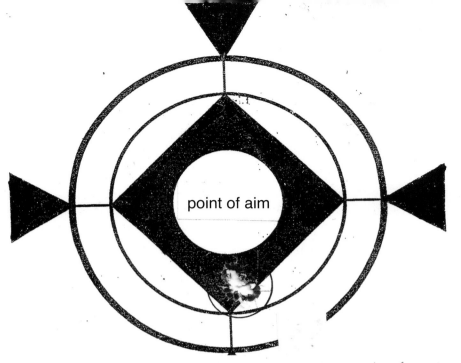

point of aim

Shot off bipod on wooden bench with sound moderator fitted

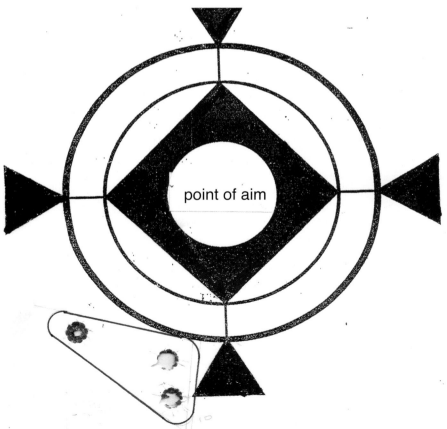

point of aim

Shot off bipod on wooden bench without sound moderator fitted

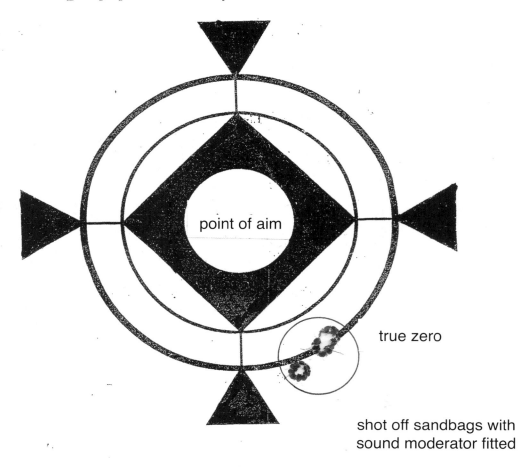

point of aim

true zero

shot off sandbags with
sound moderator fitted

c) Three shot group, centre of group 1in (2.5cm) to the right of group (a) and ½in (13mm) lower. Centre to centre group error ⅝in (16mm) (the shot slightly low and left was a 'pulled shot', in other words operator error).

These results were particularly interesting for several reasons, notably that the group shot without the sound moderator struck the target lower than when it was fitted. Usually the opposite is the case, but as we shall see, in this instance the method of support had an effect.

What might be termed true zero for most uses is actually represented by target (c) when supported by rabbit ear sandbags with the rifle held in the conventional manner at both pistol grip and forend. This then means that zeroed off the bipod as (a), the group has actually shifted left and slightly high, although the group size is very good. This shift left is exaggerated without the sound moderator fitted, as shown by group (b).

Conclusion: A wooden bench constructed from ¾in (19mm) thick plywood is not the most sturdy support, as shown by the difference between targets (b) and (c). Without the sound moderator fitted and held only at the pistol grip, the rifle bounced quite badly on the bench. This could be seen due to the right foot of the bipod lifting off the bench at each shot. Fitting the sound moderator with this rifle reduced that effect but did not entirely eliminate it as compared to shooting from a firmly rested position.

It should be noted that results may differ, but the principle of zeroing the rifle in the manner in which it is most likely to be used, and the choice of a suitable support, is important for best accuracy.

Penetration Testing

Penetration testing has the benefit of being able to observe, and therefore learn, quite a bit about terminal performance as well as being fun. I remember as a lad shooting into the end of a log with a .22 rimfire rifle, then 'sectioning' it with a small axe to see how far different velocity loads with both hollow point and solid bullets penetrated. Just for the record, low velocity solids (of what make I can no longer remember) gave the best penetration, while some high velocity hollow points gave the least, as the rapid expansion limited the penetration.

There used to be a test that the military was fond of, which entailed shooting into a box packed with 1in (2.5cm) pieces of pine. When sectioned and placed back together these would show not only the full penetration, but also the path taken through the wood by the bullet,

Plastic milk containers set up for simple comparative penetration testing.

.223 bullet striking water containers.

*.308 bullet striking water containers exhibiting a greater explosive effect
(relative to the size of the container) than the .223.*

Modest spray of water from the .450 bullet strike but excellent penetration.

A neat entry hole in a target post at 30 yards (27m), the sleeve from a modified .410 cartridge case stuck on the outside of the hole.

The rear of the wooden target post showing where the shot has passed right though it.

octagonal-barrelled, modern-built 1874 Sharps falling-block rifle (with fixed forend) appears to make so little difference that it is not noticeable. Yet my Lee Speed BSA in .303 British with the same sort of fitting well in front of the forend and a long, slim-profiled 'whippy' barrel is adversely affected, especially if there is tension on the sling.

The other external pressure point that is often given little thought is the habit some shooters have of holding the forend tightly, with the thumb of the leading hand wrapped over the barrel. What effect this has each time the rifle is fired cannot be accurately judged, but what we do know is that a) it will affect the pattern of barrel vibration, and b) it is unlikely to be the same each time, therefore we can conclude that it is not a good idea.

The rifle with suitable loads, good bullets and quality sights producing fine accuracy is a thing of joy. A combination of these elements that produces poor or, even worse, inconsistent accuracy is a recipe for despondency.

The Rifled Barrel and Lead Shot

The idea of a multi-purpose firearm, one that can be used reasonably effectively for other than its primary purpose, is always attractive, if often difficult to achieve. When it comes to the matter of successfully firing both single projectiles and shot pellets from the same firearm, we usually finish up with guns such as the Cape rifle, a side-by-side with one barrel rifled and the other smooth bore.

An alternative is the German or Austrian drilling, with two shot barrels and a rifled barrel underneath, and there are even more exotic combinations which so often tend to qualify as a solution looking for a problem. There are multi-purpose firearms with modified rifling, such as Webley & Scott's jungle gun, using straight rifling with just a twist in the last few inches. The most successful multi-purpose firearm is undoubtedly Holland & Holland's Paradox gun (now back in production) with ratchet rifling in the choke area but otherwise smooth-bored. Yet what about firing shot through a conventional rifled barrel?

Many .22 rimfire rifle users will be familiar with the shot cartridge that can be fired in both rifles and smooth bores chambered for the .22 rimfire long rifle cartridge. However, anyone who has attempted to kill a rat at more than a few feet away with this diminutive cartridge fired in a rifle will have found it to be almost useless. This is not just the disadvantage of tiny shot and a small shot load, but because the effect of the rifling is to spread the pattern.

Shot cartridges are available for use in revolvers where that type of firearm is permitted, and at one time even for the venerable Colt 1911 A1 .45 calibre semi-automatic pistol (or 'self-loading pistol' in British parlance). Wartime 'survival cartridges', described as 'for use in hunting small game, effective range 25 feet', were issued, though in this instance the distance quoted, just over 8 yards (7m), was probably rather optimistic.

Experiment

This experiment was to investigate the effects of shooting shot cartridges in a rifle with
a) the shot exposed to the rifling,
b) the shot enclosed in a sleeve.

Equipment: Ruger No. 1 .45-70 rifle.
Ammunition:
a) Loaded with ⅝oz no. 6 shot and 38 grains Swiss no. 2 black powder.
b) Cartridge loaded the same with the shot contained in a plastic sleeve made from a .410 shotgun cartridge case.
Results: Testing was conducted at (a) 20ft (6m) for the unsleeved shot, and (b) 30ft (9m) for the sleeved shot.

a) Shot was spread on average 32in (81cm), leaving large gaps between pellets in the pattern.
b) At 30ft (9m) the shot and sleeve stayed together, acting as a single projectile. Retested at 30 yards (27m), a few stray pellets hit the target but most stayed in the sleeve. Accuracy proved to be surprisingly good as a single projectile, and penetration through 2in (5cm) of pine was impressive, with the plastic sleeve concertinaed on the entry side, the shot having torn a hole to exit the wood.

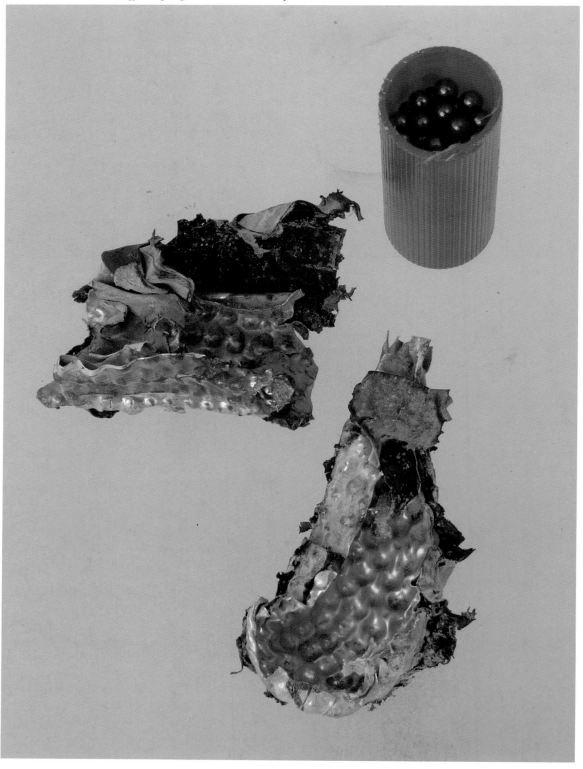

Shot sleeve made from the body of a .410 cartridge case and foil shot sleeves that failed in use.

Note: Further tests with split sleeves, and later, low velocity loads to reduce the spin rate with larger shot and heavier shot loads, gave some small improvement, although results tended to be somewhat erratic. Aluminium foil sleeves tested by a friend also keenly interested in this project gave some small improvement but tended to rupture along the joint.

Conclusion: The spin imparted by the rifling will always produce much larger shot patterns than those fired even from a smooth-bore barrel without any choke. However, the sleeved shot loads could serve a useful purpose for the humane dispatch of animals where reasonable penetration was required along with a reduction in over-penetration and a reduced tendency to ricochet (shot pistols are sometimes used for this very purpose). The benefit of the sleeved shot in a rifled barrel would be the extra distance at which it could be used, which may be important when dealing with an injured wild beast.

Chapter 5
The Smooth-Bore Gun

Often to the enthusiasts of the rifled firearm the smooth-bore gun seems quite simple, even crude technology. Considered just as a smooth-bore musket, this may at least be partly true, but the shotgun is another matter: not inferior technology, just different. After all, while the rifle maker strives for ever tighter groups, the gunmaker will endeavour to get the best shot patterns. Admittedly to outsiders, work on shotgun barrels to obtain good shot patterns seems more of an art form than subject to exact calculation, and certainly predicting results is often more difficult; experience does count for a lot, and like rifled arms, different ammunition will give varying results.

This can be particularly frustrating when a cartridge that throws good patterns in one barrel of a double gun does not perform so well in the other. With older guns this may sometimes be traced to later and perhaps less skilled work carried out in the bores, especially around the choke area. Getting really good results is always an interesting exercise with a number of variables including powder, wad type and material, and velocity, all of which contrive to have an effect on the end results, plus the barrel bore shape and dimensions. While, as with most things, there are basic guidelines, there is no ready-made formula: sometimes it is just a case of 'suck it and see'. However, before getting to the ballistics it is necessary to understand certain basics about bore sizes, choke, patterns and shot.

BORE SIZES

I have already touched upon how shotguns are gauged, a method of comparative measurement that goes back several hundred years. Just to recap, this is based on a spherical lead ball that fits the bore, and the number of these that go to make up one pound in weight. So, for example, a 4-bore would just take a 4oz ball, there being 16oz to one pound (1lb), so a 16-bore is sixteen to the pound, each weighing one ounce (1oz).

There are exceptions; for example, the fourten is a direct bore size, really a calibre rather than comparative gauge size. Also with some of the really big, smooth-bore sporting guns, usually punt guns, some sizes have letter designations. Then it becomes a little more complicated still, because there are subdivisions of each size which were for years expressed as vulgar fractions – for example $^{12}\!/_{1}$ – and different bore sizes compared to the chambering. This did not, of course, occur with muzzle loaders, where the true proof size would be stamped on the barrel and wads cut to suit. Herald in the breech loader, and we find guns with 13-bore barrels chambered 12-bore, while a 6-bore (as a muzzle loader) simply became one of the smaller gauge sizes of a breech-loading 4-bore. While many bore sizes have only a few subdivisions, the 8-bore breech loader has nine bore sizes for proof purposes.

Later sizes were marked in multiples of thousandths of an inch, so 12-bore became 0.729in, and a 20-bore 0.615in, with a size range on either size. From 1989 we also have the metric system, which is not in such fine increments as the old British Imperial system.

Bore Sizes

Bore	Size (inches)
A	2.000
B	1.938
C	1.875
D	1.813
E	1.750
F	1.688
1 (one)	1.669
H	1.625
J	1.563
K	1.500
L	1.438
M	1.375
2	1.325
O	1.313
P	1.250
3	1.157
	1.052
4	1.026
	1.001
	0.976
	0.957
	0.938
	0.919
8	0.903
	0.888
	0.873
	0.860
	0.847
	0.835
	0.824
	0.813
	0.803
10	0.973
	0.784
	0.775
	0.763
	0.751
12	0.740
	0.729
	0.719
	0.710
14	0.701
	0.693
	0.685
	0.677
16	0.669
	0.662
	0.655
	0.649
	0.637
20	0.626
	0.615
	0.605
	0.596
24	0.587
	0.579
	0.571
	0.563
28	0.556
	0.550
	0.543
.410	0.415
	0.410
	0.405
.360	0.360
	0.350

CHOKE

Choke is a restriction in the bore at the muzzle, designed to concentrate the shot charge into a smaller area than would otherwise be obtained by a cylinder-bored gun. Historically the basic idea and original patent can be traced to Pape of Newcastle, although credit for much of the later development work goes to W. W. Greener, the Birmingham gunmaker. Like many successful ideas there are other claimants, even in America, but actual proof in many of these instances appears to be lacking.

Degrees of Choke

Choke used to be measured by the old gunmakers as so many 'points', which translates into thousandths of an inch: so, for example, ten points of choke = ten thousandths of an inch on the diameter. What might be described as the standard divisions of choke are as follows:

There are also other subdivisions sometimes

Standard Divisions of Choke

Restriction	British Designation	American Designation
0.000in	True cylinder	Cylinder
0.005in	Improved cylinder	—
0.010in	Quarter	Improved
0.020in	Half	Modified
0.030in	Three-quarter	Improved modified
0.040in	Full	Full
0.045/0.050in	Extra full	Extra full or 'turkey' choke

Gunsmith's comparator in use, comparing the main bore size to the choke.

used by the gunmaker or gunsmith, such as:

0.003in	Light improved cylinder
0.007in	Tight improved cylinder

Also expressions are sometimes used such as 'tight half/tight three-quarter' and, albeit rare nowadays, 'modified half', meaning 'tight half'.

Percentage of Pellets within a 30in (75cm) Circle

However, this is only when expressed as a mechanical measurement; the real measurement of choke is the result on the pattern plate or pattern sheet, being the percentage of pellets within a 30in (75cm) circle at various distances.

Distance in yards/30in circle

Choke	20	25	30	35	40	45	50	55	60
True cylinder	80%	69%	60%	49%	40%	33%	27%	22%	18%
Improved cylinder	92%	82%	72%	60%	50%	41%	33%	27%	22%
Quarter	100%	87%	77%	65%	55%	46%	38%	30%	25%
Half	100%	94%	83%	71%	60%	50%	41%	33%	27%
Three-quarter	100%	100%	91%	77%	65%	55%	46%	37%	30%
Full	100%	100%	100%	84%	70%	59%	49%	40%	32%

Distance in metres/75cm circle

Choke	20	25	30	35	40	45	50	55
True cylinder	75%	63%	53%	43%	35%	28%	22%	18%
Improved cylinder	85%	74%	64%	53%	43%	34%	27%	22%
Quarter	90%	80%	70%	58%	48%	39%	31%	25%
Half	97%	86%	76%	64%	54%	43%	34%	27%
Three-quarter	100%	93%	83%	70%	58%	47%	38%	30%
Full	100%	100%	90%	74%	62%	51%	41%	32%

Information supplied by Eley Hawk Ltd and reproduced with their kind permission.

The percentage can be worked out quite easily; for example:

32g (1½oz) no. 5 shot – 248 pellets

So quarter choke at 30 yards (27m) should give $77 \times \frac{284}{100} = 190.96$, or 191 pellets in the 30in circle.

This does not take into account poor, patchy or blown patterns, all of which will have an adverse effect on the pellet count.

To be able to work out the correct percentage of shot within a 30in (75cm) circle, it is necessary to have a guide to the number of shot pellets relative to shot and charge size, as listed below:

Average number of lead shot pellets relative to load and shot size

Weight of shot		Size of shot							
Ounce	Gram	3	4	5	6	6.5	7	8	9
1⅝	46	228	276	356	439	492	552	726	944
1½	42.5	210	255	330	409	455	510	670	872
1¼	36	175	213	275	338	385	425	568	739
1³⁄₁₆	34	166	202	261	321	363	404	536	698
1⅛	32	157	191	248	304	342	383	504	657
1¹⁄₁₆	30	149	181	234	287	321	361	473	616
1	28.5	140	170	220	270	305	340	450	585
¹⁵⁄₁₆	26.5	131	159	206	253	284	319	418	544
⅞	25	122	149	193	236	268	298	395	513
²⁷⁄₃₂	24	118	143	185	227	257	286	379	492
¹³⁄₁₆	23	113	138	179	219	246	276	363	472
⅝	17.5	87	106	138	169	187	212	276	359
⁹⁄₁₆	16	78	96	124	152	171	191	252	328
⁷⁄₁₆	12.5	61	75	97	118	134	149	197	256
⁵⁄₁₆	9	44	53	69	84	96	106	142	185

Information supplied by Eley Hawk Ltd and reproduced with their kind permission.

Another quick and easy way to check the choke results, although a little less accurate, is to measure the diameter of the bulk of the shot charge at a given distance. Around 20 yards/metres is a good distance, because a conveniently sized, transparent hand-held gauge inscribed with concentric rings can be used.

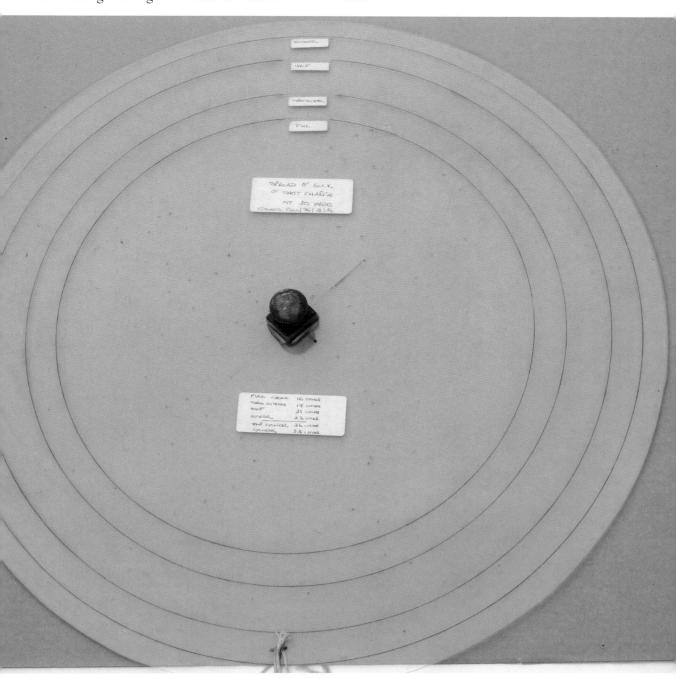

Choke gauge based on measuring the size of the bulk of the shot pattern at 20 yards (18m). Each inscribed ring gives the approximate degree of choke.

Diameter of shot spread (bulk of shot charge) at different distances

Degree of choke	Distance in yards, shot spread in inches						
Distance	10	15	20	25	30	35	40
True cylinder	20	26	32	38	44	51	58
Improved cylinder	15	20	26	32	38	44	51
Quarter	13	18	23	29	35	41	48
Half	12	16	21	26	32	38	4
Three-quarter	10	14	18	23	29	35	42
Full	9	12	16	21	27	33	40

Degree of choke	Distance in metres, shot spread in centimetres					
Distance	10	15	20	25	30	35
True cylinder	54	71	88	105	122	140
Improved cylinder	38	55	72	89	106	124
Quarter	34	49	64	80	97	115
Half	31	44	58	73	90	108
Three-quarter	27	39	52	66	82	101
Full	23	33	45	59	75	94

Information supplied by Eley Hawk Ltd and reproduced with their kind permission.

Shot Spread relating to Choke and Bore Size

It often comes as a surprise to many shotgun users to find that the spread of shot is not influenced by the actual gauge or bore size of the gun. Within an inch or so the patterns will be the same size relative to the amount of choke. In other words, small gauge guns do not shoot tighter patterns due to their reduced bore size, nor do larger guns throw particularly big patterns.

Take, for example, a 12-bore loaded with 1¹⁄₁₆oz (30g) no. 6 shot compared to a 20-bore loaded with ⅞oz (25g) no. 6 shot, both fired out of quarter-choke barrels and the results recorded at 30 yards(27m), an average kill distance:
12-bore – 1¹⁄₁₆oz (30g) no. 6 shot = 287 pellets

So quarter choke at 30 yards (27m) should produce:

77 (% of shot) $\times \frac{287}{100}$ pellets = 220.99 (221) pellets in a 30in circle

20-bore – ⅞oz (25g) no. 6 shot = 236 pellets

77 (% of shot) $\times \frac{236}{100}$ pellets = 181.72 (182) pellets in a 30in circle

Therefore for the same quarter choke at the same distance the 20-bore delivers:

$\frac{182}{221} \times 100 = 82.35$ per cent of the 12-bore pellet count, a reduction of 17.64 per cent.
If we take this a step further and go to a 28-bore with ⁹⁄₁₆oz (16g) shot load with the same quarter choke at again 30 yards, the difference in pellet count will be even more dramatic:

⁹⁄₁₆oz (16g) no. 6 shot – 152 pellets
77 (% of shot) $\times \frac{152}{100} = 117.04$ (117) pellets in a 30in circle
$\frac{117}{221} \times 100 = 52.94\%$ of the 12-bore shot load

With only just over half the number of pellets compared to the 12-bore for the same 'space in the sky', this obviously leaves a lot bigger gaps between the pellets (pattern density).

ENERGY

Pellet energy is sometimes a little overlooked by some shooters, with the desire to produce 'thick' patterns being seen as the ultimate need. Some years ago the use of open chokes and no. 7 shot was much in favour for pheasant shooting, but as with a rifle, the energy of the projectile is important, especially regarding performance and penetration at or near the maximum distance. Ultra-high pheasant shooting (the moral arguments of which are outside the scope of this book)

has brought with it the realization that larger shot and bigger loads of shot are necessary for adequate longer range performance. The larger shot retains energy better and the increased shot load contributes towards pattern density. The logic of this is, of course, nothing new to the keen wildfowler.

The drop in energy as the distance from the muzzle increases is, of course, due to air resistance, gravity and the resulting loss in velocity.

From the tables below it can be seen that for pheasant shooting the once popular no. 7 shot, even at a typical 'kill' distance of 30 yards (27m), has 'lost' $871-731 = 140\text{ft/sec}$ (42m/sec) velocity over ten yards, a drop of 16 per cent, with a drop in energy of $\frac{1.52\text{ft/lb}}{2.16\text{ft/lb}} \times 100 = 70.37$ per cent (retained), a loss of 29.629 per cent.

Striking energy in ft/lb for individual pellets, typical muzzle velocity 1,070ft/sec (326m/sec)

Shot size			Distance (yards)			
	20	30	35	40	45	50
BB	12.4	10.3	9.24	8.25	7.38	6.56
3	5.79	4.48	3.92	3.43	2.99	2.59
4	4.68	3.54	3.08	2.66	2.30	1.97
5	3.52	2.60	2.23	1.90	1.61	1.36
6	2.80	2.03	1.71	1.44	1.20	1.01
7	2.16	1.52	1.27	1.06	0.86	0.70

Information supplied by Eley Hawk Ltd and reproduced with their kind permission.

Velocity loss out to fifty yards, muzzle velocity 1,070ft/sec (326m/sec)

Shot size			Distance (yards)			
	20	30	35	40	45	50
BB	942	860	815	770	729	688
3	915	804	753	704	657	612
4	905	788	735	683	635	587
5	893	768	711	656	604	555
6	883	752	691	634	579	528
7	871	731	667	606	475	496

Information supplied by Eley Hawk Ltd and reproduced with their kind permission.

By comparison over the same distance no. 5 shot loses 893–768 = 125ft/sec (38.5m/sec) velocity, a drop of 13.9 per cent, energy $\frac{2.60}{3.52} \times 100 =$ 73.9 per cent (retained), a loss of 26.1 per cent.

As with a rifle bullet or any moving object, mass plays a big part in the retention of energy.

SHOT PELLET SIZES

The pellet size determines the mass, whether lead, steel or other 'non-toxic' shot, and shot sizes in the UK range from the largest LG to the smallest no. 9, sometimes called dust shot. To qualify under UK law as a shotgun cartridge, rather than fall into the category of section one firearms ammunition, a cartridge must contain five or more shot pellets of no more than .360in diameter.

The figures given in the table below are UK sizes. Some other countries have their own standards for sizing; the two that we are increasingly likely to encounter are the metric and American; the latter is also used in Sweden.

SHOT – ALTERNATIVES TO LEAD

Lead is the ballistically superior material for shot pellets, and that is part of the reason it has been with us for so long. Where lead is prohibited the two alternatives that come close to the ballistic performance of lead are tungsten matrix, manufactured from fine tungsten powder and polymer resin, and bismuth alloyed with tin. Tin shot has been used but is inferior in all areas of performance, and this and the tungsten and bismuth shot all suffer from being very expensive, with greater demands for the raw material for other manufacturing purposes, with a consequent high price.

One advantage of bismuth shot compared to other non-lead alternatives is that it is not harmful to barrels and can be used with fibre or felt wads without the need for a plastic shot cup. However, due to the expense at the time of writing the future for these alternatives to lead do not look good.

Steel shot is at the moment the only commercially acceptable alternative to lead shot based on price but is markedly inferior in all areas of

Shot Pellet Sizes (UK)

Sizes	diameter		number of pellets	
	inches	mm	per oz	per 10g
LG	.360	9.1	6	2
SG	.330	8.4	8	3
Special SG	.300	7.6	11	4
SSG	.270	6.8	15	5.5
AAA	.200	5.2	35	12.5
BB	.160	4.1	70	25
1	.140	3.6	100	36
3	.130	3.3	140	50
4	.120	3.1	170	60
5	.110	2.8	220	78
6	.100	2.6	270	95
7	.095	2.4	340	120
7½	.090	2.3	400	140
8	.085	2.2	450	160
9	.080	2.0	580	210

Information supplied by Eley Hawk Ltd and reproduced with their kind permission.

Other Standards for Sizing

British	metric	American
LG	9.1	-
SG	8.4	00 buck
Special SG	7.6	1 buck
SSG	6.8	3 buck
AAA	5.2	4 buck
BB	4.1	air rifle
1	3.6	2
3	3.3	4
4	3.1	5
5	2.8	6
6	2.6	-
7	2.4	7½
7½	2.3	8
8	2.2	-
9	2.0	9

Information supplied by Eley Hawk Ltd and reproduced with their kind permission.

performance and places a limit on what type of shotgun may be used. Ways of increasing the performance by upping the muzzle velocity and even using cubic shot to inflict more terminal damage have been tried. However, one cannot escape the reality that, being nearly 20 per cent less dense than lead and (even in a thick-walled plastic cup wad) harder on the barrels, also ballistically inferior, especially at the longer ranges, it is not, and cannot be, a direct substitute. The general rule applied when using steel shot is to go up two shot sizes to reclaim some of the energy that would be 'lost' compared to using smaller-sized lead shot.

One of the problems that we then run into is that by increasing the pellet size the air resistance in flight also increases by a proportionate amount. Another drawback is that using a larger, less dense material means that in order to get the equivalent shot load of both weight and number of pellets, the volume within the cartridge case has to be increased.

To overcome the deficiencies of steel shot one answer is to increase the velocity; however, this is only a partially successful answer as air resistance increases, and we are still dealing with individual pellets lacking in that important matter of size relative to mass. Imagine, for example, a solid rubber ball and another thick-walled but pneumatic ball of the same weight but necessarily of greater diameter. Thrown at the same velocity the smaller solid ball will travel further than the larger diameter ball due to less air resistance. Also steel shot rarely patterns as well as lead, and there are limitations with most shotguns on the amount of choke that can be used, often no more than half, although with new guns development work is resulting in tighter chokes for steel shot. One obvious drawback using steel shot is that it limits the effective range when compared to lead.

Unfortunately politics and an increasing clamour from organizations hostile to live game shooting is serving only to muddy the waters. So far, after several hundred years' use, there seems very little, if any, direct evidence that the use of lead shot is harmful — other than to the quarry!

Chapter 6
Smooth-Bore Ballistics

Having explained in some detail the basic elements that contribute to affect shotgun performance it is time to look at what happens from the moment of firing until the shot hits, or as is sometimes the case misses, the target. Whether that is for clay pigeon or live bird shooting or some other purpose, the parameters concerning performance are much the same. Firstly, though, it is necessary to understand the internal design of the shotgun barrel.

THE BARREL

With the conventional breech-loading gun we have the chamber followed by a short taper section, known as the forcing cone, leading into the bore, and at the muzzle usually some degree of choke. The chamber may look parallel, but it is tapered to aid extraction, and the chamber forcing cone, which is really the leed (the older spelling is usually applied to shotguns), acts a little like a funnel into the actual bore. The bore may be parallel or nearly so, depending upon the method of machining used to finish it, and at the muzzle there is usually some degree of choke, or with newer guns often a facility for a screw-in choke.

There are variations, of course. In recent years there has been a move towards longer forcing cones, sometimes extending well into the first few inches of barrel. There are many claims, some perhaps a little extravagant, as to the benefits of the long forcing cone, which we shall come to later.

Older barrels tend to be tapered a few thousandths of an inch, when they were finished by a process known as spill boring. This system used

paper or card 'liners' to adjust the setting of the tool, and would compress a tiny amount as the tool travelled up the bore. The effect is small, often only between 0.001-0.003in on the diameter, but this small taper or 'tightening' of the bore is regarded as beneficial in producing good shot patterns.

The true straight-taper bore, or 'ordinary bore' as it was sometimes called in the nineteenth century, is rare, but has recently been rediscovered by a leading gunmaker. The most extreme early example of a 'tapered' bore was the Vena Contracta, which took this idea a step further, being chambered 12-bore but having a curved section of bore reducing down to 20-bore. One example of a true straight-taper bore gun that I was fortunate to both examine and shoot was a John Perrins of Worcester dating from around 1880, which the owner described as a 12/16. Chambered 12-bore, in front of the chamber it tapered straight to the muzzle, the equivalent of full choke as a mechanical measurement, that is, 0.040in. It produced the equivalent of half-choke patterns, but only with a careful choice of wad.

Barrels without choke and a nominally straight bore qualify as true cylinder, but some degree of choke is usually beneficial in producing tidy shot patterns. Muzzle loaders do not normally have any choke, and modern-made reproductions really are true cylinder. Originals, however, may be bored in a variety of ways. Described as relief boring, they can be found slightly larger at the muzzle, which is certainly an aid to loading, or larger at the breech end, and even a combination of both, producing a sort of shallow hourglass shape. Larger at the breech end would, in its day, have been

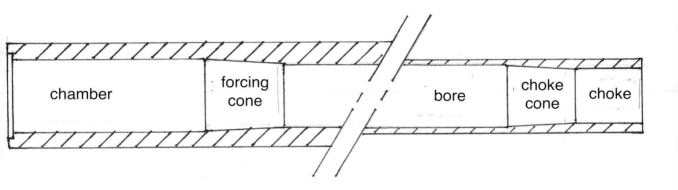

The standard internal barrel profile is chamber, forcing cone, then a straight cylindrical bore followed by the choke cone and choke.

described as 'open behind', larger at the muzzle 'open in front', and presumably a barrel tight at some point down in the bore would have been described as 'open forward and behind'. Gunmakers were noted for their simplicity of descriptive terms.

As for the actual construction of choke, the industry standard is the short choke at the end of the barrel. This has a taper section, or again a forcing cone, from the main bore into a parallel restriction, and with subtle variations can be found in both fixed and screw-in choke forms. The other rare form of choke is a recessed choke, which is a method of introducing choke into a cylinder-bored barrel as long as there is sufficient wall thickness to accommodate it. With this sort of choke the bore is opened out just before the muzzle for several inches in length so the shot column and wad expands into this larger part of the bore and is then restricted prior to the muzzle. There are limits, however, as to the effectiveness of this sort of choke, about half choke being the practical maximum. It is not completely unknown to find muzzle loaders with a recessed choke, although the usual suspicion is that it has been added sometime later.

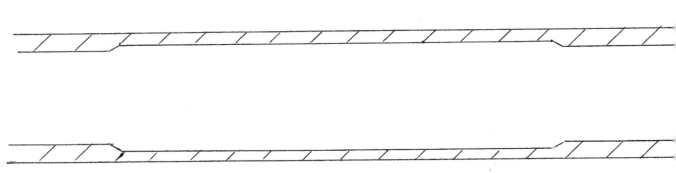

RECESSED CHOKE

Recessed choke can be introduced into a barrel if there is sufficient wall thickness.

INTERNAL BALLISTICS

As with a rifle cartridge, from the moment the firing pin (called a striker on an English gun) hits the primer to the shot charge leaving the barrel, similar basic principles apply. The cartridge is driven forwards a tiny amount, depending upon the headspace, and the primer ignites, and then starts to push back out of the cartridge case. As the powder burns and pressure starts to build, the cartridge case pushes back against the breech face (the standing breech on an English double), reseating the primer, and the sides of the cartridge case expand to grip the chamber wall and form a seal.

The shot column and wad enter the forcing cone in front of the chamber, and again as in a rifle, a steep angle at this point will produce slightly higher pressures than a shallower angle.

Similarly a shotgun that is bored 'on the tight side', meaning one of the smaller sizes within the permissible gauge sizes, will operate at a pressure a little more than one that is 'slack' in the bore.

The wad then acts as a piston, accelerating the shot column up the bore; the peak pressure point with smokeless powder is around 25 to 30mm from the breech face, but this will vary a little depending upon the powder rate of burn, and the actual internal design and dimensions of the barrel. At the choke we have a restriction, and while there may be a very small pressure surge (especially if using black powder), at this point the main load is mechanical, squeezing down the shot column and wad to a smaller diameter before it leaves the muzzle.

When using black powder (gunpowder) as a propellant, pressures are lower and the burn rate is not so rapid, so it is still burning further up the barrel than would be the case with smokeless powder. This means the pressure further up the barrel (in gunmaker's terms 'down the bore') is higher than for smokeless powder and can be used to test barrels that are suspect near the muzzle. If the charge of black powder is large compared to the shot load it will still be burning at the muzzle – too much, and it will be producing flames well in front of the gun. This, as with a big black-powder rifle in evening light, does look quite spectacular, but is rarely beneficial to the shot pattern.

The Passage of Shot up the Barrel

Shot will be either exposed to the barrel bore in the case of a separate conventional wad, or protected within a plastic cup, commonly called a plas-wad. At one time it was believed that the plastic cup wad produced tighter patterns: what it can do, in fact, is produce tidier patterns around the outside edges. This is because, with a conventional wad, the outside of the shot column is exposed to contact with the barrel, meaning some of the shot is abraded and leaves the muzzle no longer spherical. This makes it ballistically inefficient with a tendency to drift off course sometimes several inches from the bulk of the pattern.

When using a plastic cup wad the shot pellets are protected from the bore and do not suffer any damage (a relative term), and therefore are ballistically more efficient. Frustratingly, though, the results are not what we always expect, as each shotgun barrel shoots slightly differently depending upon the cartridge and load, so what should be a clear-cut case for improvement may not mirror the actual results.

When a cartridge is fired, shotgun barrels vibrate, more so than rifle barrels, and this can be tested by hanging a pair of barrels from the hook and striking them with the knuckle of a finger: good barrels produce a bell-like ring, and tested like this they are reacting just like tubular bells. This pleasing noise is caused by vibration, almost as if the barrels were shivering. There was a case made out in the inter-war period that

heavy-walled barrels shot better, or at least a little more consistently with a wider variety of cartridges than did thin-walled barrels.

By thin-walled we can mean down to 0.025in (sometimes less) at the thinnest point, which is usually just before the choke section. However, the overriding factor with the shotgun is ease of handling, and any gain from its having heavier-walled barrels (not only being more theoretical than practical) is more than offset by the need to be able to handle it for its intended use, and to add just sufficient to the overall weight in the gun to adequately absorb recoil.

It might seem obvious that the thicker a shotgun barrel, the greater its strength, but this is not necessarily so, and the quality of the steel from which it is manufactured is of considerable importance. By quality we mean the chemical composition, heat treatment where applicable, method of manufacture and, most importantly, tensile strength. The latter is a material test where a standard test piece of steel is pulled until it fails. Basically the figures, in tons per square inch, prior to failure give us its tensile strength. There are also miniature test pieces where a test bar has to be cut from a component part.

Steel has an elastic limit, meaning that within that limit it will return to its original shape; when it exceeds its elastic limit it starts to fail, and then breaks. Therefore it is possible to have thinner barrels using good quality, suitable steel, whereas a 'softer' steel with a lower tensile strength will need to be thicker walled in order to perform at the same pressures.

However, it is not as simple as that, because the barrel can be reduced in wall thickness as the pressure drops. Compare early black-powder barrels, both muzzle- and breech-loading, with smokeless powder breech-loader barrels. The early barrels are usually formed with a straight taper and are quite narrow at the breech, while a 'nitro' gun will be heavier at the breech, will taper down a little more quickly at first, and then flatten out to a fine taper.

The one thing that throws this out somewhat is the method of construction, and here I refer to twist or Damascus barrels. These were formed from iron and steel bound together, rather like plaiting hair, then forge-welded

A plastic cup wad holding the shot gives protection from abrasion against the barrel wall.

around a mandrel so the strips of 'plaited' iron and steel were arranged in a helical form, like a coil spring. The composition of the iron and steel, and whether the structure is coarse or finely made, affects the strength, although late Damascus barrels, very finely made and with a high percentage of steel, are the strongest, being quite suitable for use with smokeless powder.

What they all have in common is that, compared to steel, they are relatively soft, which can be seen by the fact that they dent quite easily when knocked against some hard object. Yet Damascus barrels can, at times, perform remarkably well when there is a problem, like a burst due to an obstruction, where the rupture area is limited, compared to early steel barrels, which will split alarmingly. The reason is the method of construction, where the grain of the iron and steel is wrapped around the barrel rather than laid longitudinally.

Occasionally one comes across shooters claiming a certain expertise who say they can detect, in use, the degree of vibration in any shotgun barrels. I doubt this is normally so because when the barrels are locked on to the action and the forend fitted, this all has a dampening effect, and the time taken for the shot to travel up the barrel is somewhat faster than human reactions can comprehend, even allowing for the residual lingering vibration. However, it is certainly possible to detect vibration when something is wrong, such as a loose rib or a double-barrelled gun that has not been assembled correctly.

I once had to work on an early English hammer gun with a loose top rib that exhibited very few signs of use, which seemed a bit odd considering the rib was almost hanging off. The rib was duly relaid, but when the gun was later tested it was an awful thing to shoot, even with compar-

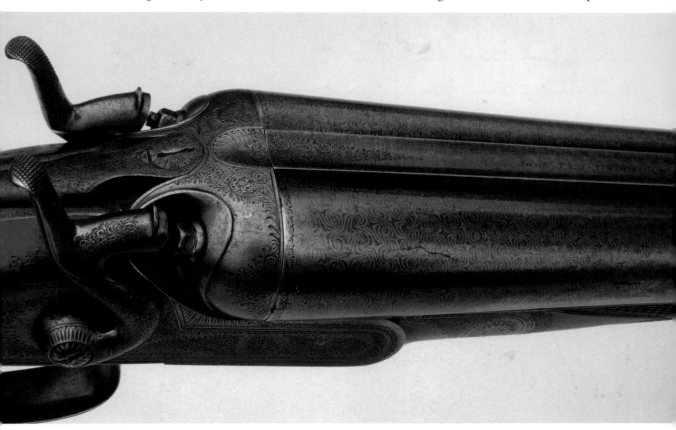

The Damascus barrel made of iron and steel bound together and forge-welded around a mandrel usually performs better in the event of a failure than early steel barrels.

atively modestly loaded black-powder cartridges. It emitted what can only be described as a high-pitched 'shriek', and yes, the barrels did vibrate, even with ribs firmly in place. The fault, it seemed, was the assembly of the barrels at the breech end where the brazing was not 100 per cent complete. There was little doubt that this gun had probably always been unpleasant to shoot, and as a consequence had received very little use, but the top rib soon became detached due to the fairly awful vibration that occurred every time it was fired.

The Effect of Choke

Choke, it was once suggested, was rather like placing your thumb on the end of a hosepipe to make the water squirt out faster and further. This is not quite the same as shotgun choke because there is no constant and large build-up of pressure, and as previously noted, the main load is mechanical, squeezing the shot column through a smaller area.

Compared to a true cylinder barrel, choke acts as a 'brake', slightly reducing the velocity at the muzzle end, and the greater the degree of choke, the more this effect. On the plus side, the shot charge from a choked barrel does not spread as rapidly as that from an unchoked barrel. Take, say, full choke and the shot charge travels a short distance, almost like a single projectile, compared to the rapid dispersion of shot from a true cylinder barrel.

The result is that the shot charge from a choked barrel initially suffers less from air resistance and therefore retains its velocity better in the early stages of flight. It is calculated that, by the twenty yard mark, velocity will then

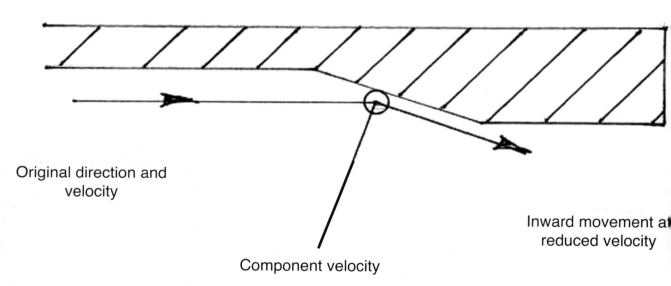

Original direction and velocity

Component velocity

Inward movement at reduced velocity

JOURNEE PRINCIPLE

The Journée principle states 'when outside pellets strike the cone of the choke they are given an additional velocity at right angles to the surface of the cone'.

be superior to that of shot fired from an unchoked barrel. In practice the variation is so small that there is no noticeable difference; the real and obvious effect is the striking power of the denser shot pattern evident from a choke barrel.

So we come to the question, if choke does not work like a hosepipe with the nozzle restriction, how does it work? The accepted explanation is the Journeé theory, which states that 'when an outside shot pellet strikes the cone of the choke they are given an additional velocity at right angles to the surface of the cone'. This means that, as well as the forward movement, there is a tendency to change direction – in this case inwards – which reduces their tendency to spread. Consider it rather like a controlled ricochet, but where the change of direction of the outside shot pellets is limited by the presence of the main shot charge.

It can be deduced from this that, while in the choke cone, the outside layer will apply a similar, albeit reduced, load on the next layer of shot pellets, and so on. The net effect is to apply an inward movement to the shot charge, helping to moderate the in-flight spread.

This brings up two interesting points: one, that the steeper the forcing cone, the more pronounced this effect; and second, the length of the choke section is of lesser importance. In practice there is a limit on the steepness of the cone, but different makers have exhibited various ideas as to the length of the choke section, some being very short but which work well. What is undesirable is a choke that is too long, say more than $1.5 \times$ bore diameter, as this then tends to reduce the 'Journeé effect'.

Some Problems

Problems usually manifest themselves as poor shot patterns, and one of the most important component parts is the wadding. With a muzzle loader it is not so important as with a breech loader, but ramming just balled-up paper over the powder charge rarely gives good results; even muzzle loaders deserve decently formed wadding, preferably well lubricated to keep the powder fouling soft.

With a breech loader one vital area is the transition from chamber to barrel via the leed or forcing cone. The wad has to be long enough to enter the cone without any tendency to tip out of line with the axis of the bore. With a cartridge that is the correct length for the chamber this is rarely a problem, and a fibre wad in the proportion of its length, being two-thirds of the diameter, will normally suffice, bearing in mind there is usually a card wad either side giving a combined measurement of the length equal to the diameter. Anything longer than this 'square' measurement is rarely necessary, although the material used will make a difference.

For example, I have made wads from the coarse, soft felt used for carpet underlay. On its own it is not effective, but two of those soft felt wads with a card wad in between and one either side works tolerably well. Before loading it is nearly one and a half times longer than its diameter, but once under some compression, it achieves nearly square proportions.

Theoretically problems may occur when the chamber is longer than the cartridge, such as using a 2⅛in (65mm) cartridge in a 2¾in (70mm) chamber gun or longer, such as a 3in (76mm). In practice, with modern materials and especially plastic cup wads, it is not a problem, although the pressure curve will be slightly different as there is less initial resistance. It is of more concern to the hand-loader, and wads that are not only short but also too hard could give a combination of tipping and gas escape into the shot column, which will have adverse effects upon velocity (and therefore energy) and the pattern.

The fashion for back-bored barrels (meaning, to older gunsmiths, oversize) and very long forcing cones increases the potential for problems with fibre wads, mainly due to gas escape up the side of the wad with, again, the potential for reduced velocities and poor patterns. Proponents of these methods claim reduced recoil and improved patterns. Certainly the former may be true, but good patterns are partly dependent upon a wad sealing correctly, and if this is not achieved the opposite may be the reality, along with reduced velocity.

It has long been argued that the ideal shot load for any gauge of gun is that which is equal

The composition and length of the cartridge wadding is important. For the keen muzzle loader or cartridge hand-loader, it is worth experimenting with a variety of wadding.

to the weight of the spherical lead ball that gives a shotgun its nominal bore size. While this might seem to be 'old hat', there is a lot of sense in it, and it takes into account other matters such as the relative weight of the gun and the effect of the felt recoil. This is often referred to as a 'square load', meaning, as with the wad, a ratio of length equal to its diameter when in the cartridge case or barrel. It is not quite true, as the size of shot, and therefore the air gaps between, makes a difference, as large shot for a given load takes up more space. That apart, one of the benefits is that an increased load used in a larger bore gun means a bigger and therefore heavier gun well suited to dampening down the recoil.

The other matter is, a long shot column in the barrel when using a fibre wad means more shot pellets exposed to potential deformation and therefore seeming ballistically inefficient. To a certain extent this is offset by the increase in the total number of shot pellets, and negated when a plastic cup wad is used. A very short shot column used to be a recipe for blown or scattered patterns, but cartridge manufacturers have now, with modern powder and wads, produced amazingly good results that were unthinkable not many years ago, and have defied many previously long-established ideas. A long shot column does, though, contribute towards a stringing of the shot pellets in flight, which is a form of inefficiency.

THE FLIGHT OF SHOT

Under normal circumstances, upon leaving the muzzle, shot behaves like a single projectile for a few yards before it starts to spread. The shot pellets most likely to spread the furthest (outside the pattern) are those that are deformed in some way, and these, being ballistically inferior, are also the ones likely to fall behind to give an elongated shot pattern in flight – known as the stringing effect. It is commonly assumed by non-shooters that the shot pellets blast out in a cone shape, each pellet following a straight line of flight, but actually they follow a curved line of flight. Also they are subject to the law of gravity, just like a rifle bullet, although over the distance a shotgun is normally used, the effect of trajectory is not usually obvious. Most shooting with a 12-bore involves a distance of around 30 to 35 yards (27 to 32m), with 40 to 45 (37 to 41m) usually being regarded as a long shot, and for most purposes 50 yards (46m) being extreme range, even with a gun with a lot of choke.

Furthermore the laws concerning energy are, again like the rifle bullet, the same – that is, for a given velocity, larger, heavier shot pellets initially have more energy and retain it better at longer distances, while at the same time large pellets have greater air resistance. Wildfowlers tend to use bigger loads and larger shot because the quarry can be quite big and some shooting will take place at longer range than might normally be encountered in the field. The limiting factor is not only that of individual pellet energy, but the need for multiple strikes to ensure a clean kill as there is no precise point of aim. Therefore the other matter that limits the distance a shotgun might be used at is density of the shot pattern.

Experiment

The following experiment was to check the shot spread of a .410 shotgun at different distances.

Equipment

* A .410 shotgun, 2½in 65mm cartridges containing $^7/_{16}$oz (12.5g) no. 6 shot
* Plain card sheet, shot at a) 2in (5cm), b) 3ft (90cm), c) 6ft (1.8m), d) 12ft (3.7m) and e) 18ft (5.5m)

Note: A .410 was used in order to minimize damage from muzzle blast at the shorter distances.

Results: Shot spread at a) gauge size, b) 1in (2.5cm), c) 2½in (6.4cm), d) 5½in (14cm), e) 10½in (26.7cm).

Conclusion: The results show that the shot did not follow the flight path of a straight-sided cone, but curved outwards from the line of flight as distance increased.

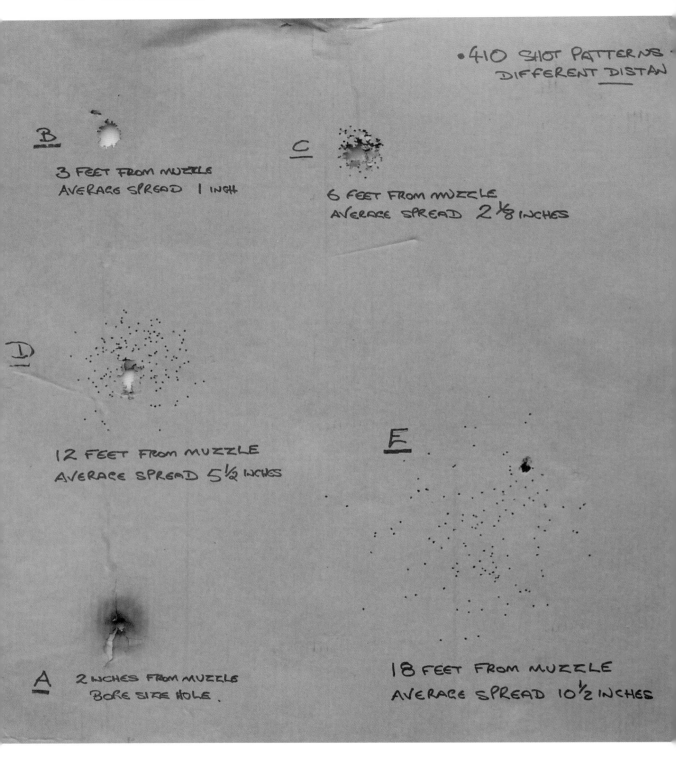

Shots taken at a plain cardboard sheet showing the shot spread at different distances with a .410 shotgun.

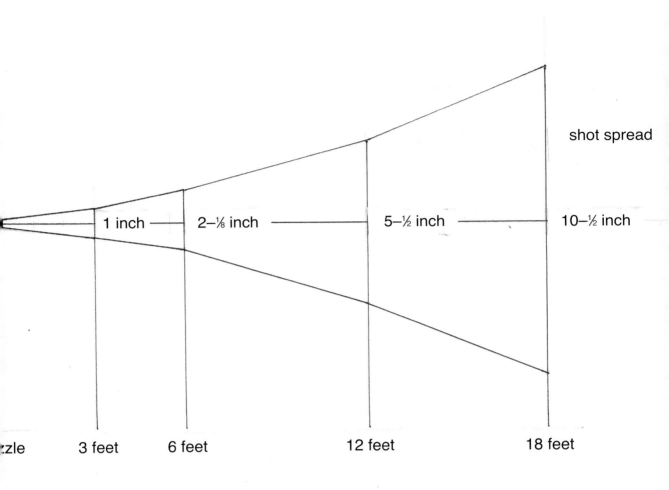

SPREAD OF SHOT FROM .410 SHOTGUN (NOT TO SCALE)

Diagram showing the increasing spread of the shot pellets in flight. This includes the fliers on the outside of the main shot pattern.

Any deficiency in the pattern may be compounded by the fact that the target, either live or inanimate, is generally moving, and may not be – and most often is not – at right angles to the direction from which the shot it taken. Also we have to consider that the shot does not arrive on target in the form of a flat disc of pellets, and is often without an even spread. These are the sorts of variable that add a degree of imprecision to shotgun shooting that is anathema to dedi-

cated rifle enthusiasts. However, it works, and the needs of the live game shooter are met by the aforementioned pellet energy and multiple strikes, the latter obtained by producing good, even patterns.

The clay shooter's requirements are a little different. Here, density of pattern, especially with a clay pigeon presented sideways on, is a necessity, but pellet energy is of lesser importance. A popular shot size for clay pigeon shooting (now often called clay target shooting) is No. 7½ shot, which for this type of sport gives a good balance between dense shot patterns and sufficient energy, not just to break the clay, but to carry far enough; in other words, to have sufficient range. No. 9 shot would seem to be an attractive proposition to give exceptional pattern density, having over 500 pellets even in a ⅞oz (25g) load. However, this 'dust shot', as it is sometimes called, while adequate on close targets, would lose velocity and energy very quickly and therefore diminish the effective range at which it could be used.

Shot Stringing

Shot stringing, as already mentioned, is an elongated shot pattern when in flight. This has an effect on terminal performance, as a shorter shot string appears to strike harder, or as an old gunsmith friend of mine put it: 'Most of the shot arrives at about the same time'. A simplification perhaps, although it has a ring of truth – but how important is this shot stringing?

Firstly it is necessary to consider what is actually happening. When in flight the shot disperses laterally, which is what gives us the spread, but as the distance from the muzzle increases, so the longitudinal spread of the pellets also increases. This happens because of imperfections in shape and weight during manufacture, and as already pointed out, abrasion of the outside pellets in the shot charge (when using fibre wads) while travelling up the bore. It follows, therefore, that in flight some pellets are ballistically more efficient than others due to subtle variations in size, shape and weight. The pattern plate, while an eminently useful tool in many respects, cannot determine any inefficiency due to stringing, as some pellets will arrive to 'fill in the gaps' a few thousandths of a second after the first strike.

With a stationary target, such as the proverbial 'sitting duck', this stringing does not present a problem, but a fast crossing bird or clay could mean a reduced amount of the shot charge having any effect. Over the years a number of practical tests have been carried out to ascertain the effect, and the conclusions are that most of the shot charge flies in a reasonably compact col-

umn with a long, thinner tail made up of about 15 per cent of the total number of pellets.

However, it may surprise the reader to find that at 40 yards (37m) the distance between the most ballistically efficient front pellet to the ballistically inefficient rear pellet can be as much as 12ft (3.7m), depending upon shot charge, size and velocity. At, say, 1,000ft/sec (305m/sec) this then means a time difference of twelve thousandths of a second, so for most practical purposes the time lag will have no great effect.

The concern at longer ranges with live game shooting is that because of the increasing tendency for the pellets to string out, as well as disperse laterally, the loss of energy from the more ballistically inefficient pellets will result in loss of penetration. Once again, tests conducted over the years have shown that at 30 yards (27m) all of the shot charge for any given purpose (size of game to size of shot pellet) is effective. At 40 yards (37m) this drops to 95 per cent, while at 50 yards (46m) only around 50 per cent of the shot charge is fully effective, with a further 25 per cent being just below its calculated required performance figure.

In practical terms all this means is that, if shooting within effective range, the disadvantages due to shot stringing are more theoretical than practical. When it comes to pushing the boundaries past the normal limit, it is likely the shot pattern will already be so dispersed as to have an adverse effect on performance as well as an overall loss of pellet energy, which in itself limits the practical distance at which shots should be taken.

Anyone who is concerned that shot stringing, even at average kill distances of, say, 30 to 35 yards (27 to 32m), will have a noticeably adverse effect when dealing with a fast crossing bird, whether real or artificial, should consider the following: take a pheasant travelling at 40mph (65km/h) directly at right-angles to the shooter some 30 yards (27m) away and using choke that puts the bulk of the shot into a 30in (76cm) circle at this sort of distance. It has been calculated that the distance flown by the bird from the time the front pellet arrives to the last will be 11.1in (28.2cm), just over a third of the overall pattern diameter, so as long as the shot placement is correct, the bird will always be covered well by the shot pattern. Also, the time lag between the first and last pellet from a cartridge with a muzzle velocity of 1,070ft/sec (326m/sec) and striking velocity at 30 yards (27m) 752ft/sec (230m/sec), and energy of 2.03ft/lb (2.75 joules), is 0.015sec.

Pushing the distance a bird is shot to the limit, say 50 yards (46m), and there is more cause for concern. Even with full choke the pattern within our imaginary 30in (76cm) circle will contain barely half the shot charge, the rest often being quite scattered, which, with a game load of 30g (1⅛oz) no. 6 shot means:

$$\frac{\text{no. of pellets} \times 49 \text{ (\% of pellets)}}{100} = \frac{287 \times 49}{100} = 140 \text{ pellets}$$

At the same time, the shot pellets in this diminished pattern will have a striking energy at 50 yards (46m) of 1.01ft/lb (1.37 joules) velocity down to 528ft/sec (161m/sec), a shot string measuring on average 26.8in (68cm), with pellet arrival time spread over 0.038sec. Even at this, clean kills are possible with really good shot placement, but there is little room for error and it relies on the gun producing good, even shot patterns.

The answer, of course, for longer range game shooting is to increase the velocity, pellet size and shot charge. One such example would be changing to 34g (1³⁄₁₆oz) of no. 5 shot (261 pellets) with a velocity of 1,120ft/sec (341m/sec) and using full choke. The number of pellets within our 30in (76cm) kill zone will be reduced to 128, but velocity would be 574ft/sec (175m/sec), and energy nearly a third more at 1.46ft/lb (1.98 joules). The shot string will be little different, and the total pellet arrival time marginally improved. The most important factors are a reasonably dense pattern and increased striking energy for each individual pellet.

Whatever we do there are practical limits to the performance of the shotgun, although increasing the velocity, shot load, pellet size and gauge of gun are advantageous in the search for extra performance. However, the law of diminishing returns will soon come into play, where eventually any gain in performance is no longer proportional to what is applied to get a small advantage.

Shot Patterns

In an ideal world the pattern of shot as seen on a pattern sheet or plate, would be circular in form with a completely even distribution of pellets – but this is rarely, if ever, the case. What we find acceptable as a good shot pattern can be a compromise between practical reality and perfection. We usually settle for approximately the right number of pellets for any given choke, of reasonably even distribution, perhaps concentrated towards the centre and sufficiently close to ensure multiple strikes on the target.

Poor patterns, by contrast, can be patchy with a very uneven distribution of pellets; they may be 'blown', meaning wildly scattered and inconsistent from shot to shot, or even 'cartwheel', where there are few pellet strikes in the centre of the pattern but a sort of halo or thick band of pellets around the outside, representing, with a bit of imagination, the rim of a cartwheel. This pattern is rare.

The reasons for poor patterns can be many, including badly bored barrels, poorly formed or unfinished chokes, or a make and load of cartridge that does not perform at its best in a certain gun, reason often unknown but nonetheless a fact of life. The cartridge load, wadding and, in the case of older designs, the overshot card, can interfere with achieving a good pattern. Realistically most modern cartridges from reputable makers perform reasonably well; it then becomes a matter of matching a cartridge to a particular gun to get the best shot patterns.

At first checking a pattern can seem a bit confusing, but there is a simple and systematic approach to this matter. Checking concerns two areas: firstly the number or density of pellets within a circle at, usually, 40 yards (36m), which tells us what the choke in the gun is actually producing; and secondly the evenness, or otherwise, of the spread of the shot.

Counting the number of pellets can be done in two ways: either by shooting at the traditional painted steel pattern plate and drawing a circle around the bulk of the pellet strikes, or using dedicated pattern sheets divided into drawn segments. When using the first method it is best to mark off pellet strikes in easy to add up multiples, such as fives. The traditional 'tool' for this

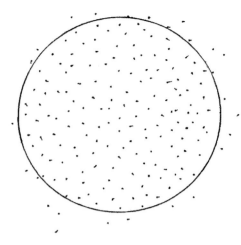

The ideal even pattern

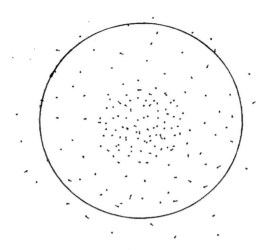

Pattern concentrated in the middle. A hard-hitti
pattern for the good shot

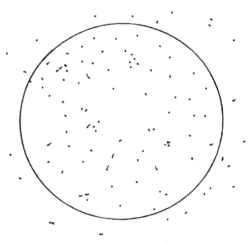

A poor pattern, with clumps of
pellets and large gaps

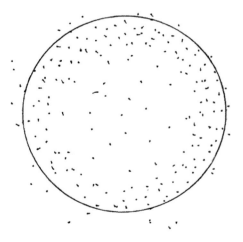

The rare and undesirable
'cartwheel' pattern

Shot patterns. The ideal even pattern is not often found; patterns are usually a compromise.

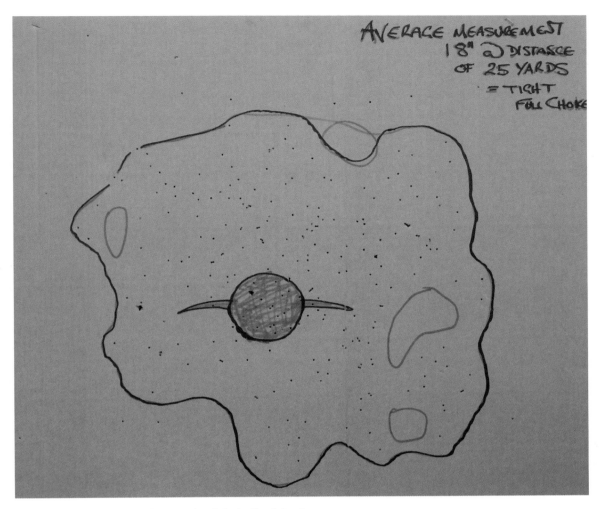

'Joining the dots' around the outside of the bulk of the shot pattern is an interesting exercise. With an aiming mark it also indicates, as in this case, whether you are shooting straight or off to one side.

marking up was a spent shotgun cartridge case with the open end flattened. With a dedicated pattern sheet it is very easy to count the strikes in each segment, then add up the total.

On the pattern plate with its sticky paint coating the shot pattern can be observed or photographed if need be, but there is a limit to what can be done. By contrast the pattern sheet can be taken from the shooting ground for examination at leisure, and the best way to observe the actual pattern is to turn it around to the plain back of the sheet.

An even pattern is fairly obvious, and one way of getting a better impression is to 'join the dots' around the outside of the pattern, but ignoring those odd fliers some distance from the strikes of the main shot charge. With a scattered pattern it can be an interesting exercise to draw around each clump of shot, ignoring those more than, say, 3in (7.6cm) apart, so you finish up with what appears to be a collection of strangely shaped 'islands'. The alternative is to 'join the dots' in areas within the pattern without pellet strikes to highlight those blank patches. Identifying elements of poor shot patterns is a bit of fun, but the main object of the exercise is to learn enough to be able to judge good patterns easily.

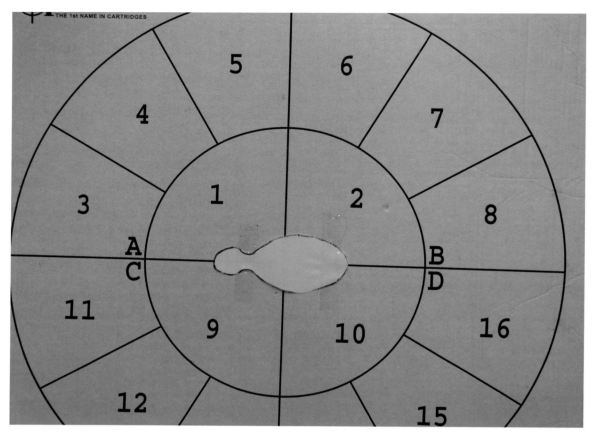

A bird profile of the vital areas is useful in judging the killing potential of a pattern. In the absence of anything more sophisticated, paper stick-on profiles can be used.

Another checking method of interest is to have cut-outs of bird profiles, less feathers. This only needs to be a basic dumbbell shape, and if made from a see-through material such as Perspex, it can be moved around the pattern sheet to get an idea of those areas of the pattern that represent a good number of pellet strikes relative to the bird size, and those parts that may be deficient. Once again I have to emphasize that this is not exactly the same as true life with all the variables, but it is the best we can do, and good shot patterns are a vital element in successful shotgun shooting.

The Big Pattern

So far we have concentrated on most shotgun shooters' dream, the idea of extending the range for effective shooting, but there is another role for the shotgun, that of ultra close-range shoot-

ing for sports such as rabbits dodging between bushes only a few yards away. This means being able to produce at 10 to 20 yards (9 to 18m) the kind of shot patterns we would normally associate with shots taken at 30 to 40 yards (27 to 36m), dependent upon the choke used. In the past, various 'spreader' devices have been used, but probably the most effective method is to exaggerate the aerodynamic spread by using shot pellets of a ballistically inefficient shape. For this you cannot get much more ballistically inefficient than by using cubic shot. It certainly works, the spread being increased by as much as 50 per cent. FN once produced a cartridge named the Dispersante which fulfilled this role very well.

Experiment

This experiment was to make a comparison between cubic and spherical lead shot.

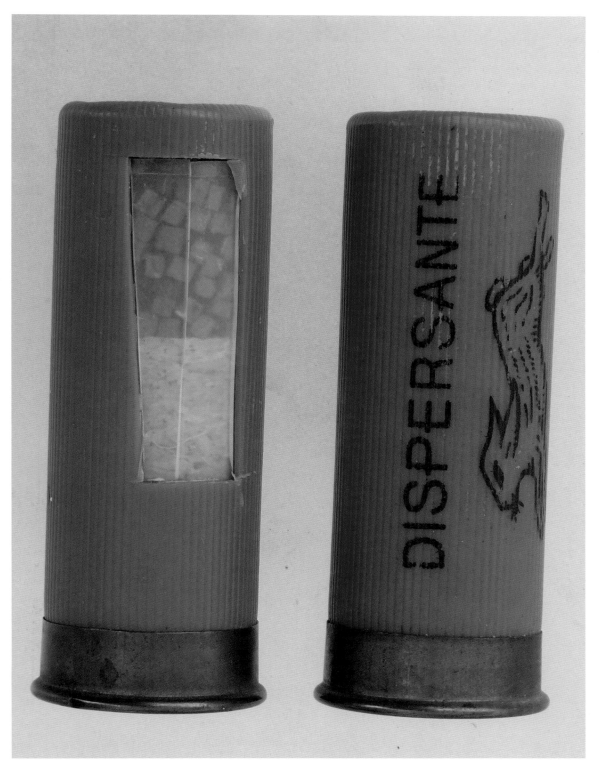

An old but usable FN Dispersante cartridge, the left-hand example cut away to show the cubic shot.

Equipment: A shotgun with full choke (as measured). FN Dispersante (cubic shot) cartridges, nominally no. 6 shot size, and conventional game cartridges with 1⅛oz (30g) no. 6 shot.

Results: Testing at 25 yards (23m) gave the following results:

* Dispersante cartridge: fairly good, even spread, the bulk of the shot within a 31in (79cm) circle.
* Conventional game cartridge: all the shot within a 21in (53cm) circle.

Retested at 40 yards (36m), the pellet count for the spherical shot was 68 per cent nearly true full choke (70 per cent), and the pellet count for the cubic shot 15 per cent.

Conclusion: The cubic shot, due to its inefficient ballistic shape, does spread more rapidly than spherical shot. At 25 yards (23m), which is the kind of practical maximum distance at which it might be used; the pattern with the FN cartridges in this particular shotgun was quite good.

At 40 yards (36m), regarded as the usable maximum for a 2½in game cartridge, the spher-

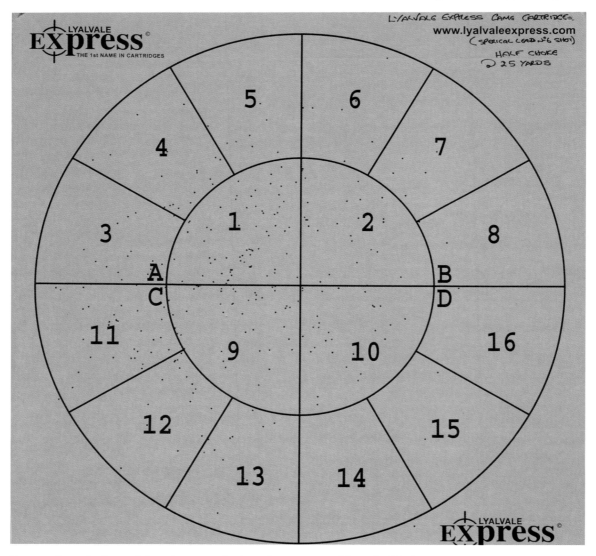

Pattern sheet of spherical shot showing a fairly tight pattern at 25 yards (23m).

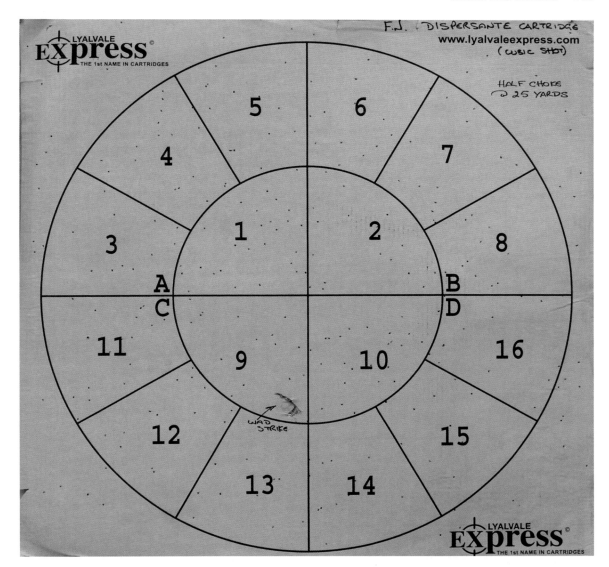

Pattern sheet with cubic shot for comparison with spherical shot, also shot from the same barrel at 25 yards (23m).

ical shot showed its superiority. The other limiting factor with cubic shot will be a more rapid loss of velocity and therefore pellet energy due to the increased air resistance. However, for its intended use, such as rabbits dodging between bushes at very close range, the cubic shot could be the best choice.

Note: A recent development with cubic shot is the Winchester Blind Side (as in duck blind) cartridge. This is a 3in (76mm) cartridge loaded with what Winchester describe as hex shot, meaning 'six-sided'. It is steel cubic shot with rounded corners. The performance of the No. 3 shot was limited to around 40 yards (36m) due to both its ballistically inefficient shape and lack of mass for its size (less dense than lead). Even at that distance it had a tendency to shoot low, indicating a drop in velocity. What was impressive was the wad cup used, which held the shot together for far longer.

Tested in a suitable half choke gun and for comparison against Eley Alphamax magnum the following results were recorded:

* Winchester Blind Side, 1⅜oz (40g) no. 3 cubic steel shot (pellet count virtually equivalent to 1⅝oz (46g) no. 3 spherical lead shot). Percentage of shot within 30in (76cm) circle at 40 yards (36m) – 45 per cent.
* Eley Alphamax magnum 1⅝oz (46g) no. 3 spherical lead shot. Percentage of shot within 30in circle at 40 yards – 50 per cent.

The lead shot cartridge will have a greater range due to its ballistic superiority, but the control of spread of the steel cubic shot due to the special cup wad was a considerable advance in cubic shot technology. The Winchester wad used with spherical lead shot, where permitted, could be the basis of an excellent wildfowling cartridge.

SHOOTING SOLID PROJECTILES FROM A SMOOTH-BORE GUN

At some time or other the idea of shooting solid projectiles with reasonable accuracy from a smooth bore comes to mind, but is this even possible? In the late 1970s I was loaned a Durs Egg duelling pistol made in the traditional British manner without rifling and was surprised at its accuracy, albeit only at ten paces. However, it is generally accepted that smooth bores are grossly inaccurate, as the ball has a tendency to skid and bounce down the bore, meaning it does not leave the muzzle in quite the same direction from shot to shot. However, my experience with the duelling pistol gave me cause to question this theory.

Further to that, a few years ago I made a powder test mortar for a teaching establishment in which the length of the bore was the same as the

This scaled-down powder test mortar with 2in (50mm) bore and firing steel balls was surprisingly accurate.

diameter of the steel ball with which it was loaded. With an accurately measured powder charge, which sat in a chamber recess behind the ball, it exhibited good accuracy, dropping the 2in (50mm) steel balls close together out to around 90 yards (82m). Of course, in this case the ball had little chance to skid or bounce, as once it started to lift, after moving only half its diameter, there was no longer contact between ball and bore, and the bore was lapped to fit the ball very accurately. It was noted that the best accuracy was obtained with the faster burning powders, which never exceeded the maximum charge of 40 grains.

Experiment

The following experiment was to test the accuracy of ball shot from a smooth bore.

Equipment: Modified Pedersoli reproduction Brown Bess musket, 0.750in bore diameter, 1oz swaged lead balls, 0.730in diameter +/− 0.0015in, lubricated patches 1⅜in diameter (lubricant 50:50 tallow and beeswax), 0.010/0.012in thick. Card wad between ball and powder. Powder charge 90 grains Swiss no. 4 black powder, distance 50 metres (54 yards).

Results: Even allowing for the primitive sighting arrangements of simply lining up the target across the barrel and a small foresight bead, accuracy was disappointing. Results were erratic, and it was not possible to predict where each ball might strike the target. Some fliers were attributed to the lubricated patch sticking to the bullet (even after it had passed through the target board and into the sand), in that a sticking patch could cause uneven drag. Slightly better results were obtained with a dry patch, underneath that a soft lubricated wad and thick card over the powder.

A firearms student experiencing firing the flintlock musket during the solid ball tests.

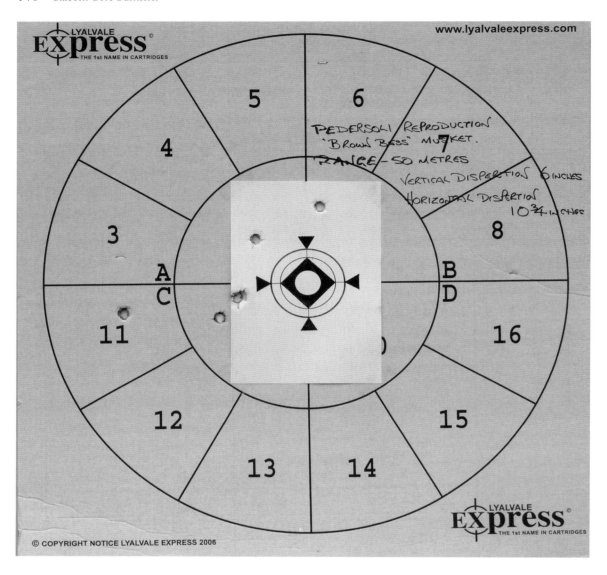

The target shows handwritten notes:

PEDERSOLI REPRODUCTION
"BROWN BESS" MUSKET.
RANGE – 50 METRES
VERTICAL DISPERSION 6 INCHES
HORIZONTAL DISPERSION
10¾ INCHES

The results on target were disappointing because the areas where the ball might strike proved to be unpredictable.

Conclusion: With a good parallel bore and careful loading, at 50 yards (46m) it would have been possible for the British soldier to hit a man-sized target – somewhere! It is also equally likely he could miss an officer and his horse at 100 yards (90m), especially where speed of loading was more important than precision of loading. The inaccuracy in this test could not be attributable to the 'last bounce of the ball in the bore' as is often promoted, because that was eliminated by the close-fitting patch. The sticking patches may, however, give a clue. Even though every effort was made to ensure they were loaded concentric with the muzzle and bore, those that adhered to the ball did not always do so in the centre of the ball relative to the axis of the bore, and therefore line of flight. In other words, they caused drag to one side.

Even the swaged balls used were of slightly imperfect shape, and propelled out of a smooth bore there is no spin to stabilize them around their centre of gravity. The imperfect shape

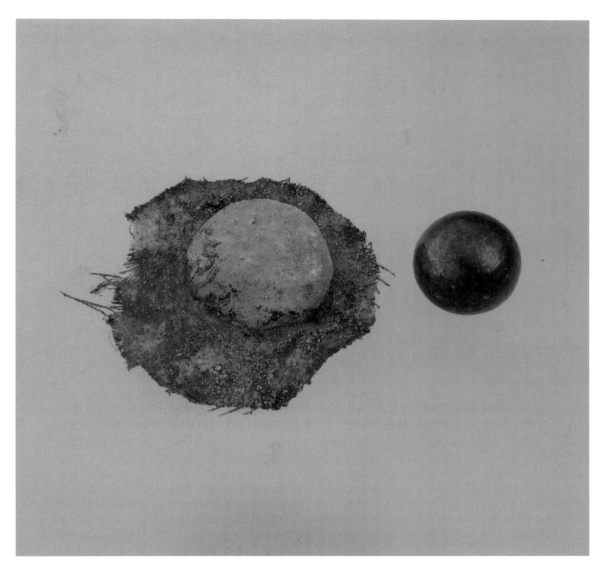

Some inaccuracy was attributed to lubricated patches sticking to the ball and causing uneven drag. This patch was still stuck after passing through the target, backing board and into the sand bullet catcher. There is an unfired ball on the right for comparison.

means an imperfect air flow, which in turn means the low pressure area behind the ball (even with a subsonic projectile) and its tail may not be in line to the projected line of flight – and this, in the same way as the sticking patch, but to a lesser extent, will tend to drag the ball off course. The quite good results achieved with the powder test mortar might be attributed to the lack of a patch, the close-fitting lapped bore, and the steel ball being truly spherical.

The idea of solid projectiles in smooth-bore guns also brings up the use and relative accuracy of rifled slugs. Here there are a number of variables, including actual size of the slug, whether or not a wad is fitted, and even, with that type, the tightness of the screw used to hold the wads on to the slug. Then there are matters such as the bore size of the shotgun and the degree of choke, if any. Having discussed this with a manufacturer of rifled slug cartridges, for consistent

The short-barrelled shotgun with 'red dot' optical sight used in the rifled slug tests.

results they recommended using a cylinder-bored shotgun for the testing I proposed, while another claimed some choke was beneficial.

Experiment

The following experiment was to test for accuracy a batch of 12-bore rifled slug cartridges, from a distance of 50 yards (46m).

Equipment: A double-barrel 12-bore modified with quarter rib and fitted with 'red dot' optical sight. Barrels 24¼in. Bore measurements: right barrel 0.721in (18.3mm), left barrel 0.718in (18.2mm), right barrel choked improved cylinder.
Ammunition: Remington Slugger, slug diameter 0.695in (17.6mm), card wad, fibrous main wad with short nylon cup over the powder.

Note: Remington claim the 'Slugger' cartridge can be used with any degree of choke, but improved cylinder gives the best result. As the right-hand barrel of the test gun measured light

improved cylinder (0.003in) this barrel was used for all the testing.

Results: In a gun weighing 7lb (3.2kg) and firing from a rested position, recoil was noticeable. In most cases the cartridge main wadding was found around 15ft (4.6m) in front of the firing point, and one wad was found just short of the target. Apart from one shot which pulled off low and left (possibly the slug with a sticking wad), grouping was reasonably consistent, although accuracy in this shotgun was not outstanding. Re-testing at 25 yards (23m) gave no better than strikes up to 2in (5cm) apart.

Conclusion: This hollow slug, while not outstandingly accurate, gave more predictable grouping than the spherical ball used in the muzzle loader, and the advantage of even a simple optical sight made sighting much easier. In another shotgun with different bore and choke dimensions it is likely that the performance might be different again, either better or worse.

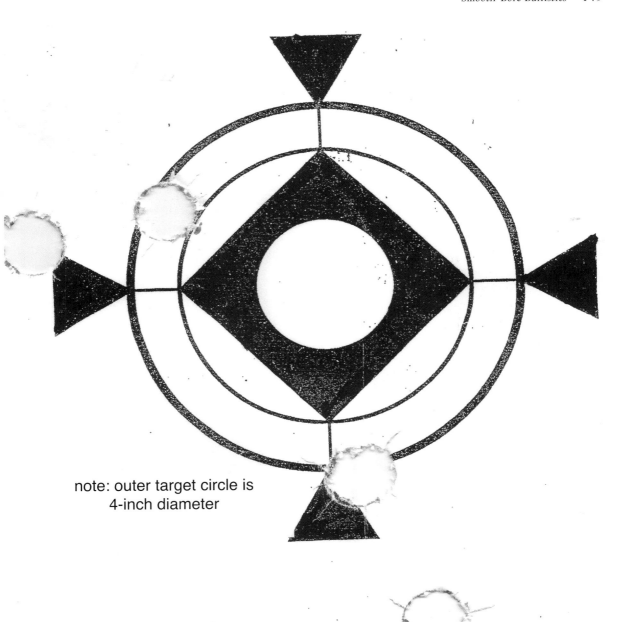

note: outer target circle is
4-inch diameter

RIFLED SLUG SHOT AT 50 YARDS

Four-shot group shot at 50 yards (46m). The strike low and right may have been caused by a wad sticking to the slug. Further tests at 25 yards (23m) produced strikes at between 1½ and 2in (4 and 5cm) from each other, usually in an L-shaped pattern.

The expansion of this hollow slug was impressive, the penetration limited to a matter of inches when fired into soft soil. At top right is an example of the slug before firing.

Measuring the penetration of the ball from the muzzle loader after digging it out of the earth bank. It was noticeable that the balls tended to change direction and run just sub-surface for much of their length.

Comparative terminal performance: Visually, when striking a soft earth backstop the performance of the slug seemed quite dramatic, with soil thrown into the air. On close examination the soil was well broken up, and the completely expanded slugs found within 4in (10cm) of the surface. By comparison the ball from the muzzle loader would easily penetrate over 12in (30cm) of soft earth, striking at a similar angle into the bank backstop.

Glossary

RIFLE TERMINOLOGY

accuracy A measurement of precision used to describe how well or consistently a rifled firearm performs on the target.

action As in 'bolt action', a description of the assembly of parts that feed, fire and eject the cartridge, usually a basic description of how it works; another example would be 'break open action'.

action body The main part or frame of an action to which the barrel is fixed. A term usually reserved for older non-bolt action designs (with a bolt action the part that serves the same function is the receiver).

air resistance Air is composed of matter which slows the forward motion of any projectile. Air resistance increases with velocity; the relative ability of a bullet to overcome air resistance is its ballistic efficiency.

aspect ratio The ratio of a bullet diameter to length. Example: a spherical ball is 1:1; a bullet where the length is twice the diameter would be 1:2.

assembly A collection of parts operating together for a specific function: for example, trigger assembly.

ball A round lead ball which was at one time the only form of bullet. Ball ammunition used by the military is a cartridge loaded with a single projectile, even though this is not a ball, but of elongated shape.

ballistics The study of projectiles in motion. While a bullet is still in the barrel this is internal ballistics; when in flight it is external ballistics.

ballistic coefficient The indicator of the ability of a projectile to overcome air resistance, calculated from the ratio of a bullet's weight to the square of its diameter and its form factor.

ballistic drift Also sometimes called 'spin drift' or 'gyroscopic drift', it is the tendency of the bullet in flight to drift in the direction of the rifling twist.

barrel The tube through which the bullet is propelled by a charge of powder when ignited (or air, in the case of an air rifle).

ball powder Propellant powder in the form of near-spherical kernels.

bearing surface That part of a bullet that is in contact with the rifling.

belted case A cartridge case which has a raised band, the belt, forward of the extraction groove. This type of cartridge headspaces off the belt in a similar manner to a rimmed cartridge.

black powder Also known as gunpowder, and the only propellant in use for hundreds of years. Made from charcoal, sulphur and potassium nitrate (saltpetre), it is still in use today with vintage firearms and modern reproductions of the same.

boat tail A design of bullet where a short section behind the bearing surface tapers to the base.

bolster That part of a percussion rifle (or shotgun) into which the nipple is screwed.

bolt action A method of breech closure by the longitudinal movement of a cylindrical bolt.

bolt face The front of the bolt against which the head of the cartridge rests.

bolt stop A projecting lug which limits the backward travel of the bolt.

bore The inside of the barrel. In a rifled firearm the bore is the original (smooth bore) dimension before the rifling is cut, and the size is the calibre.

bottleneck case A cartridge case having a neck of reduced diameter to the body similar to the shape of a bottle.

bourrelet According to the *Oxford English Dictionary*, this is a 'ridge-like excrescence'. When applied to a bullet it may be used to describe the main body, or just that part of the body behind the ogive leading up to raised driving bands. While there seems to be some confusion on this matter, the latter application would appear to be more in line with the OED.

breech The rear face of the barrel, but often applied to the whole breech area including the chamber.

breech block The part that blocks the breech of a barrel and supports the head of the cartridge.

breech loader A firearm that is loaded from the breech.

breech pressure The pressure inside the chamber generated when firing a cartridge.

bullet The projectile shot from a rifled firearm.

burning rate The relative speed at which propellant powders burn.

calibre The true bore of a rifled firearm before

the rifling grooves are cut. The diameter measured across opposite lands (see 'lands' below).

cannelure An indented ring or groove around a jacketed bullet.

cartridge In its simplest form a paper tube (cartridge paper), containing ball and powder to aid loading a muzzle loader. Latterly a brass case with primer, powder and bullet, forming a complete unit.

cartridge case The main body of the cartridge.

cast bullet A bullet made by pouring molten lead into a mould.

centre-fire A type of cartridge with the primer positioned centrally.

chamber That part of the barrel that contains and supports the cartridge.

charge As in powder charge, the amount of powder used on any particular load, whether breech or muzzle loader.

combustion The burning process, which produces gas and heat.

core The material (usually lead) inside a bullet's outer metal jacket.

Coriolis effect Bullet drift due to the effect of the earth's rotation.

crimp A series of small indents or a rolled ring that engages the mouth of the cartridge case with the bullet, usually into the cannelure.

drift The movement of a bullet to the side of a direct line of flight.

drop The fall of a bullet due to a combination of wind resistance and gravity measured from its line of departure to its point of strike.

effective range The maximum distance a bullet may travel accurately and retain sufficient energy to do its job, either at a target or live game.

elevation Vertical sight adjustment to move the barrel up or down to effect the zeroing.

energy Measured as muzzle energy and calculated from bullet weight and velocity. Energy is the capacity to do work.

erosion The washing away of the bore by the action of the hot propellant gases at high velocity and pressure. A contributory factor is also friction caused by the passage of the bullet up the bore.

extreme range The greatest distance a bullet will travel. The optimum angle for rifled firearms to obtain the longest range is 34 degrees from the horizontal.

extruded primer The flow of primer metal around the firing pin indent that produces a raised ring or crater appearance usually indicative of high breech pressures.

eye relief The distance the eye needs to be from the rear or ocular lens of a riflescope to obtain the full field of view.

firearm A generic term for any shotgun, rifle or pistol from which a projectile(s) is fired by the action of hot, expanding gases from burning powder.

fireform Reforming or changing the shape of a cartridge case by firing it in a chamber of different dimensions.

fire lock In some countries used to describe a matchlock equipped with a burning fuse, in the UK it was also a term used to describe the later flintlock.

firing mechanism Those parts of a rifle that operate together, or in sequence, to detonate the primer.

firing pin That part of the firing mechanism that strikes the primer. In break-open rifles of British origin the term 'striker' is more often used.

flake powder A powder formed most often in thin flat discs and usually intended for fast burning.

flash hider/flash suppressor A device fitted to the muzzle to reduce muzzle flash, especially from the user's view.

flash hole The hole or holes leading from the primer pocket into the main body of the cartridge case. The hole(s) through which the flame from the primer ignites the main charge.

flat point Maybe a contradiction in terms, but actually a bullet design with a pronounced flat nose of a type often used in tubular magazine rifles.

flintlock An ignition system using sparks generated by a flint.

foot pounds An expression of energy or unit of work. The energy required to lift one pound weight one foot.

forend That part of the stock under the barrel forward of the receiver or action body. When full length of the barrel, or nearly so, it may be referred to as the forearm.

form factor The coefficient of reduction or multiplier that relates the shape of any bullet to the shape of a standard projectile used to produce a ballistic table.

freebore An alternative term for the lead (or leed) into the rifling.

fouling Deposits from burnt powder left in the bore after firing.

full metal jacket A bullet where the jacket is formed from the meplat to the base, the lead core being exposed only at the rear. Originally described as full patch bullets.

gain twist The type of rifling where the twist rate gradually increases from chamber to muzzle.

gas/gases The product of the combustion of propellant powders to propel a bullet or projectile through the bore of any firearm.

gas check A soft metal disc attached to the base of a cast lead or lead alloy bullet to protect it from hot propellant gases.

gauge guns Large bore rifles where the bore sizes are based on the old shotgun method of bore sizing.

gilding metal An alloy of copper and zinc used for the jackets of some bullets.

grain A unit of weight measurement based on the Imperial system and used for measuring powder and bullet weight: 7,000 grains = one pound weight.

gram A unit of weight measurement based on the metric system: one gram = 15.4324 grains.

groove diameter The diameter of a rifle bore to the bottom of the rifling grooves.

group The distribution of bullet strikes on a target with the same aiming point. Group size is measured from centre to centre of the furthest holes in the target.

gun powder The earliest propellant powder made from a mixture of charcoal, sulphur and saltpetre for firearms use, usually referred to as black powder.

hang fire Delayed ignition of a powder charge.

head height The measurement on a bullet from the shoulder of the ogive to the tip or meplat.

headspace The space between the head of the cartridge and the bolt or breech face when the rifle action is closed.

heel The point where the base of a bullet meets the bearing surface (or the angled surface of a boat-tail bullet).

hollow point An opening or blind hole in the front of a bullet to aid rapid expansion.

jacket The metal envelope or outside covering of a bullet.

joule A unit of measurement. 1 joule = 0.7376ft/lb.

jump The extent to which the axis of the rifle bore rises due to recoil while the bullet is still travelling down the barrel.

keyhole The elongated hole left in a target struck by an unstabilized bullet that is tumbling.

kick A common term used to describe recoil; it includes other factors than just recoil including various thrusts imparted by the shape of the stock.

lands The raised part of the rifling: measurement across the lands is the true bore diameter or calibre.

large bore A term normally used to describe a rifle of at least .450in calibre. A .577 is large bore, or what some enthusiasts would call 'big bore'.

lead/leed The tapered bore in front of the chamber leading into the rifling; may also be described as the freebore.

leading Lead (from a plain lead bullet) which adheres to the barrel from the passage of the bullet; this usually occurs if the velocity is too high for the type of bullet, or a lead/alloy mix that is too soft.

line of departure A line projected from the axis of a rifle bore.

line of sight (LOS) The line from a shooter's eye over or through the sights to the target.

loading density The ratio or volume of powder charge to case capacity.

lock time The time between tripping the trigger mechanism and the firing pin striking the primer.

meplat The diameter of the blunt end at the tip of a bullet – noticeable on full metal jacket bullets, while ballistic tip bullets are truly pointed.

metal fouling The deposit of metal from the jacket of a bullet in the rifling, something that is detrimental to accuracy.

minute of angle (MOA) A minute of angle is 1in at 100 yards (it is actually 1.0471680in).

misfire A cartridge that does not fire after the primer has been struck.

mouth The open end of a cartridge case.

mushroom/mushrooming The shape of a bullet that has struck animal tissue or similar where the front has expanded to produce a shape similar to a mushroom.

muzzle The front end of the rifle barrel from which the bullet emerges.

muzzle blast The release of gases from the muzzle following the bullet.

muzzle energy (ME) A calculation of the energy of a projectile from its weight (mass) and velocity just in front of the muzzle: $ME = \frac{WV^2}{450240}$

muzzle flash The visible effect (usually in poor light) of the burning gases in front of the muzzle after the bullet leaves the barrel.

muzzle loader A rifle loaded via the muzzle.

muzzle velocity The velocity of a bullet usually measured in feet per second just in front of the muzzle.

neck The forward part of the cartridge case that holds the bullet.

nipple A tapered small bore tube with a screwed end that fits on to the bolster or drum (if a drum and nipple conversion) of a muzzle loader, on to which is fitted a percussion cap for ignition.

nock form The major diameter of a barrel that fits against the receiver or action body. Not all barrels have a nock form.

ogive The radiused section at the front of a bullet – the head of the bullet.

patch A piece of lubricated cloth around the ball of a muzzle loader. With an elongated bullet used in either a muzzle loader or breech loader it is a 'paper-patched bullet'. Early copper-jacketed bullets were described as 'copper-patched'.

percussion cap A top hat or cup-shaped hollow copper cap containing a fulminate, which ignites when struck. Used as the means of ignition for percussion muzzle loaders and capping breech loaders.

percussion rifle A rifle designed or adapted to be fired using the percussion cap for ignition.

point of aim The point at which a rifle's sights are aimed or aligned.

point blank The distance a bullet will travel before it needs sight adjustments to compensate for trajectory, generally used to mean a shot fired so close to the target that no sighting is necessary for effective aiming.

pressure The force generated inside a barrel and expressed in pounds per square inch (psi).

primer/priming charge The small powder charge which ignites the main powder charge, the assembly of cap, primer and anvil that is used in a centre-fire cartridge known as a Boxer primer. The similar Berdan primer has no separate anvil, this being formed at the bottom of the primer pocket in the head of the cartridge case.

primer pocket The shallow hole or cavity in the head of the cartridge case where the primer is seated.

projectile In relation to rifles meaning a bullet; however, a bullet does not in reality become a projectile until it is actually in flight.

proof The test of a firearm's strength to withstand test pressures in excess of normal service pressures to establish its structural integrity.

propellant Powder burnt to produce gases to propel a projectile.

receiver That part of a rifle that houses the breech closing mechanism and into which the barrel is fitted. In older designs it is more often referred to as the 'body' or 'action body'.

recoil The backward thrust of a rifle caused by the reaction to the forward thrust of accelerating the bullet up the bore with the burning powder charge. Newton's law – to every action there is an equal and opposite reaction.

reticule Cross hairs or sighting point in a riflescope used for aiming purposes. The American spelling is 'reticle'.

ricochet A bullet in flight which has glanced off a hard surface and changed its direction of flight. This is sometimes accompanied by a 'buzzing' noise when the bullet in flight after the ricochet is unstable.

rifling The spiral form in a bore to impart spin to a bullet and provide gyroscopic stability.

rimfire A cartridge with the priming compound inside a hollow rim.

rimless cartridge A common description used to describe a cartridge using a case of the recessed rim design.

rimmed cartridge A cartridge case design with a raised rim of bigger diameter than the case body.

rotation The spin of a projectile in line with its axis, imparted by the rifling.

round-nosed Used to describe a bullet with an ogive of half its calibre.

sear A lever between the trigger and cocking piece to provide controllable leverage to release the firing mechanism.

seating depth The depth a bullet is seated into a cartridge case. For convenience this is usually measured by the overall length of the assembled cartridge.

secant ogive A bullet design in which the cylindrical bearing surface of the bullet is secant to the curve of the head.

sectional density The ratio of a bullet's weight to the square of its diameter.

semi-rimmed cartridge A cartridge using a case where there is a recessed rim but the rim diameter is slightly larger than the case body but not as pronounced as a rimmed cartridge.

shock The transfer of the kinetic energy of a bullet to animal tissue or other soft medium.

shock wave The atmospheric disturbance produced by a bullet travelling faster than the speed of sound; the noise generated by a supersonic bullet in flight.

shoulder The sloping or curved part of a bottleneck cartridge case below the neck.

sight A device for aiming a firearm, either an open-sighted (V and post) aperture, or optical magnifying types.

sighting The process of aiming.

sight radius The distance between front and rear 'open sights'.

smokeless powder A high energy powder used as a propellant.

soft point A jacketed bullet with an exposed lead tip.

spin The rotation of a projectile imparted by the rifling.

spire point bullet A pointed bullet design primarily for longer range use. See also 'secant ogive'.

spitzer bullet A pointed bullet, usually of the tangent ogive type.

stabilize The rotation of a projectile around its axis sufficient to keep it point forwards in flight.

tangent ogive A bullet where the cylindrical bearing surface is tangent to the curve from the point of the bullet.

throat *See also* 'lead (leed)' or 'freebore': the tapered start into the rifling.

time of flight The time it takes for a projectile or bullet to cover a given distance.

trajectory The curved flight path of a bullet.

twist The rate the rifling turns in the barrel expressed as a number of turns in so many inches, or turns measured in calibres.

velocity The speed of a projectile or bullet usually measured in feet per second (fps).

windage Horizontal sight adjustment.

yaw The deviation of a bullet in its longitudinal axis from a straight line.

zero The sight setting where the point of bullet impact and point of aim are the same.

SPECIFIC SHOTGUN TERMINOLOGY

action body That part to which the barrel(s) fits, and with a boxlock holds the lock mechanism.

barrel tubes The barrels of a shotgun may be referred to as tubes, but this is normally used to describe the barrels as component parts prior to assembly.

bore The inside of the barrel, also used to denote the size, for example 12-bore, although the older term for size was 'gauge', still used in the USA. Bore can also be used to describe an operation, as in 'to bore a barrel'.

breech The end of the barrel into which the cartridge fits.

choke A restriction before the muzzle end of the barrel, which has the effect of concentrating the shot pattern.

Damascus Barrels produced by forging together iron and steel which, when suitably treated with chemicals, exhibits distinctive patterns.

forcing cone/lead-in/leed The taper from the front of the chamber to the bore of the barrel.

gape The amount a break-open gun has to open at the breech to allow loading.

gauge The bore size of a shotgun based, for most sizes, on the number of lead balls of a diameter to fit the bore that make up one pound in weight.

Journée effect The explanation of how choke works: 'When an outside pellet strikes the cone of the choke they are given an additional velocity at right angles to the surface of the cone.'

pellets Small lead balls graded in different sizes for use in shotguns. Alternative materials include steel, soft iron, tin and various tungsten-based compounds. Also may be described as shot or shot pellets.

shot pellets *See also* pellets. In rare instances shot pellets may be other than spherical; one example is cubic shot, designed to maximize spread.

shot stringing The longitudinal spread of shot pellets along the flight line.

shot pattern The vertical and horizontal spread of shot seen as a pattern on a pattern sheet or plate.

smooth bore A term used to describe a firearm without rifling; a gun, as in shotgun; also a musket.

Index